Tiziano Scarpa was ... ...et, novelist, playwright ... ... a number of acclaimed ... ... *Broiler* and *Western Kamikaze*. ... play *Popcorn* received international critical acclaim and was aired by the BBC and other European radio stations. He regularly speaks at creative writing conferences and writes as a journalist for national newspapers. In 1997 he won the 49th Italia Prize for his writing. He lives in Venice.

'To write originally about Venice must be one of the greatest challenges a writer can take up. Every year, hundreds of books on the city are published, but none resembles this one... Scarpa warns his readers to beware the lethal "aesthetic radioactivity" projected by the buildings and paintings of Venice. I fear his sharp eye and quick ear can only make that bewitching disease more acute, helped by Shaun Whiteside's felicitous translation' *Independent*

'A gorgeous tribute to one of the strangest and most beautiful cities on Earth. Was it Henry James or Mary McCarthy who said, "There is nothing new to say about Venice"? Tiziano Scarpa has proved them both wrong' Erica Jong

Tiziano Scarpa

 · *Venice is a fish*

A guide

Translated by Shaun Whiteside

A complete catalogue record for this book can be obtained from the British Library on request

The right of Tiziano Scarpa to be identified as the author of this work has been asserted by him in accordance with the Copyright, Designs and Patents Act 1988

First published as *Venezia E' Un Pesce* in 2000 by Giangiacomo Feltrinelli Editore Milano

First published in this edition in 2009 by Serpent's Tail
First published in this translation in 2008 by Serpent's Tail,
an imprint of Profile Books Ltd
3 Holford Yard
Bevin Way
London WC1X 9HD
website: www.serpentstail.com

ISBN 978 1 84668 728 0

Designed and typeset by Sue Lamble

Printed and bound by
CPI Group (UK) Ltd, Coydon, CR0 4YY

10 9 8 7 6 5

V ENICE IS A FISH. Just look at it on a map. It's like a vast sole stretched out against the deep. How did this marvellous beast make its way up the Adriatic and fetch up here, of all places? It could set off on its travels at any time, it could call in just about anywhere, following its fancy: it could migrate, travel, frolic as it has always liked to do: Dalmatia this weekend, Istanbul the day after next, summer in Cyprus. If it's anchored hereabouts, there must be a reason for it. Salmon wear themselves out swimming against the current, climbing waterfalls to make love in the mountains. Sirens and swordfish and seahorses go to the Sargasso Sea to die.

Other books would laugh at what I'm telling you. They speak of the birth of the city from nothing, its resounding commercial and military success, its decadence: poppycock. It wasn't like that, believe me.

Venice has always existed as you see it today, more or less. It's been sailing since the dawn of time; it's put in at every port, it's rubbed up against every shore, quay and landing-stage: Middle Eastern pearls, transparent Phoenician sand, Greek seashells, Byzantine seaweed all accreted on its scales. But one day it felt all the weight of those scales, those fragments and splinters that had permanently accumulated on its skin; it felt the weight of the incrustations it was carrying around. Its flippers grew too heavy to slip among the currents. It decided to climb once and for all into one of the most northerly and sheltered inlets of the Mediterranean, and rest there.

On the map, the bridge connecting it to terra firma looks like a fishing-line: Venice looks as if it's swallowed the bait. It's doubly bound: a steel platform and a strip of tarmac; but that happened afterwards, just a century ago. We were worried that Venice might one day change its mind and go off travelling again; we fastened it to the lagoon so that it wouldn't suddenly get it into its head to weigh anchor and leave, this time forever. We tell everyone else we did it for its own protection, because after all those years in its moorings, it's lost the knack of swimming: it would be caught straight away, it would end up on some Japanese whaling ship, or on display in a Disneyland aquarium. The truth is that we can no longer do without it. We're jealous. And even sadistic and violent, when it comes to keeping someone we love. We've done something worse than tying it to terra firma: we've literally nailed it to the sea bed.

In a novel by Bohumil Hrabal there's a child who's obsessed with nails. He constantly hammers them into the floor: at home, in a hotel, when visiting other people's houses. All the parquet floors that come within his reach are hammered away at from dawn till dusk. As though the child wanted to fix the houses to the ground, as a way of feeling more secure. Venice is made just like that; except that the nails are made not of iron but of wood, and they're enormous, between two and ten metres in length, with a diameter of twenty or thirty centimetres. They're planted in the slime of the seabed.

These buildings that you see, the marble *palazzi*, the brick houses, couldn't have been built on water, they would have sunk into the mud. How do you lay solid foundations on slime? The Venetians thrust hundreds of thousands, millions of poles into the lagoon. Underneath the Basilica della Salute there are at least a hundred thousand; and also at the feet of the Rialto Bridge, to support the thrust of the stone arch. St Mark's Basilica rests on big oaken rafts, supported by elm-wood stilts. The trunks were floated down to the lagoon along the River Piave, from the Selva di Cadore on the slopes of the Venetian Alps. There are larches, elms, alders, pines and oaks. La Serenissima was very shrewd, she always kept a close eye on her wooden possessions; the forests were protected by laws of draconian severity.

Upside-down trees, hammered in with a kind of anvil hoisted on pulleys. I had the chance to see them as a child: I heard the songs of the pile-drivers, sung to the rhythm of the slow and powerful percussion of those cylindrical mallets suspended in the air, running on vertical rails, slowly rising and then crashing back down again. The trunks are mineralised precisely because of the mud, which has wrapped them in its protective sheath, preventing them from rotting in contact with oxygen: breathless for centuries, the wood has been turned almost to stone.

You're walking on a vast upside-down forest, strolling above an incredible inverted wood. It's like something dreamed up by a mediocre science-fiction writer, and yet it's true. Let me tell you what happens to your body in Venice, starting with your feet.

 · *feet*

V ENICE IS A TORTOISE: its stone shell is made of grey trachite boulders (maségni in Venetian), which pave the streets. All the stone comes from elsewhere: as Paolo Barbaro has written, almost everything you see in Venice comes from somewhere else, it's been imported or traded, if not actually plundered. The surface you are treading on is smooth, although many of the stones have been beaten with a small milled hammer to keep you from slipping when it rains.

Where are you going? Throw away your map! Why do you so desperately need to know where you are right now? OK: in all cities, in the commercial centres, at bus stops or underground stations, you're used to having signs that hold you by the hand; there's almost always a big map with a coloured dot, an arrow to bellow at you, 'You are here'. In Venice, too, you need only look up to see lots of yellow signs with arrows telling you: you've got to go this way, don't get confused, *To the Railway Station*, *To San Marco*, *To the Accademia*. Forget it, just ignore them. Why fight the labyrinth? Follow it, for once. Don't worry, let the streets decide your journey for you, rather than the other way round. Learn to wander, to dawdle. Lose your bearings. Just drift.

Do what we call 'acting Venetian': after the war the phrase alluded to our football team, 'doing the Venetian', 'doing a Venice'. Our footballers had an exasperating, selfish style of play, always with the ball at their feet, loads of dribbling and hardly any passing, a limited vision of the game. Of course they did: they'd grown up in that varicose whirlpool of alleyways, little streets, sharp turns, bottle-necks. So obviously, even when they took to the field in shorts and jerseys, they went on seeing *calli* and *campielli* – streets and squares – everywhere, and struggled to disentangle themselves from a private labyrinthine hallucination between the midfield and the penalty area.

Imagine you're a red blood cell running along some veins: you follow the heartbeat, you allow yourself to be pumped by that invisible heart. Or else you're a mouthful of food being carried along by the intestine: the oesophagus of an extremely narrow *calle* squeezes you between brick walls until they are practically grinding you, then pushes you out, sends you slipping through the valve of a bridge that flows to the other side of the water and deposits you in a wide stomach, a *campo* from which you can't continue without first having paused for a while, forced to stop because the façade of a church holds you back, chemically transforms you to your very depths, digests you.

The first and only itinerary I suggest to you has a name. It's called: *at random*. Subtitle: *aimlessly*. Venice is small, you can afford to get lost without ever really leaving it. At the very worst, you'll always end up at the water's edge, looking out over the lagoon. There is no Minotaur in this labyrinth, no aquatic monster waiting to devour its victims. An American friend of mine came to Venice for the first time one winter night. She couldn't find her hotel, and with mounting anxiety she roamed the whole of the deserted city, clutching a pointless piece of paper bearing its address. The more minutes that passed, the more convinced she became that she was bound to be raped. She was astonished to have spent three hours in a strange city without being attacked, without anybody running off with her luggage. This was a girl from Los Angeles! Keep an eye out for pickpockets, particularly around St Mark's Square, and on crowded jetties. If you can't find your way you'll always meet a Venetian who'll be happy to show you how to double back. That is, if you really want to.

Getting lost is the only place worth going to.

You can wander confidently around, anywhere, at any hour of the day or night. There are no rough parts of town, or rather there aren't any left: the only possible nuisance might be the occasional drunk. Incidentally, start familiarising yourself with the words of Venice: the districts aren't called *quartieri*, as in other Italian cities, but *sestieri*, because there are six rather than four districts in the historic centre: each one of them is a sixth of Venice, not a quarter like the four groups of buildings that form in cities thrown up at the crossing of two major roads, in the four slices of earth cut by a crossroads. Santa Croce, Cannaregio, Dorsoduro, San Polo, San Marco, Castello. The house numbers on the doorposts don't start at 1 on each street, but continue to count the whole *sestiere*. The *sestier de Castello* reaches the record number of 6828, in Fondamenta Dandolo, at the foot of the Ponte Rosso. On the other side of the same bridge, at the end of Calle delle Erbe, the *sestier de Cannaregio* begins, with its quota of 6426.

The paving stones are set one behind the other, in long segmented lines. They mark the direction of the *calli*, emphasising their lines of perspective. The city planners clearly designed them especially for children, who like to walk without standing on the dividing lines between one stone and the next. 'Don't cross the line!' said Salvador Dalí, summing up the compositional laws of his painting, so formally reactionary, and so insane in the content of its vision. Did being a child in Venice mean getting used to not crossing the lines, respecting the outlines of forms, while upsetting their contents? Do Venetian feet pretend to bow to the status quo while at the same time giving it a visionary distortion? Do we have dazed big toes, elated heels? Look at how much surrealist delirium, what an absurd, oneiric city we have managed to produce by insanely arranging a billion perfectly perpendicular parallelepipeds! Each *maségno* is an emblem, reproducing in miniature the whole of Venice, a city stuffed into its own outline, inexorably segregated from the water, prevented from expanding, from going beyond itself, driven mad by too much meditation, too much introspection. Look how many churches you come across with every step you take. A city that is seemingly pious, in fact theologically anarchic, devoted to a plethora of major and minor saints, adherents of an exploded, disseminated, utterly lunatic religion. Each *maségno* is a coat of arms without heraldic figures, a blazon consisting solely of a grey background, a blank slate, obtuse, unmarked: the only design on this vacant escutcheon is its perimeter. But tread on them, the rows of *maségni*: you'll notice the differences in height (a few millimetres only) through the soles of your feet. One French gentleman walked on them as a child and remembered them for the rest of his life.

On the twenty-first of November, the feast of the Madonna della Salute, place yourself at the exact centre of the octagonal church, beneath the lead chandelier that plunges tens of metres from the dome; drag the sole of your foot across the bronze disc set into the floor, as tradition decrees, touch with the tip of your shoe the words *unde origo inde salus* cast into the metal: from the origin comes salvation, the origin is the earth, walking on it brings you luck, does you good; salvation rises up from the feet. You should learn to make the sign of the devil with your toes, to discharge the gesture into the earth, letting it run the whole length of your body.

Apart from the inevitable mess left by man's best friend, it's only at the Zattere, in the springtime, that you need to watch where you put your feet: some Venetians go there to fish at night, using lamps and torches to attract enamoured cuttlefish and catch them in a kind of big butterfly net. From the bottom of their buckets, the captured cuttlefish catch you unawares by spurting ink on to the stones of the shore, staining socks and trousers.

Feel how your toes turn prehensile on the steps of the bridges, clutching at worn or squared edges as you climb; your soles brake you on the way down, your heels halt you. Wear light shoes, soft-soled, not post-punk boots or trainers with rubbery air-pockets, no spongy inner padding. I suggest this spiritual exercise: become a foot.

· legs

A SLOG: THE HOUSES ARE OLD, very few have lifts; there wasn't room in the stairwells. In the street, every fifty or hundred metres a bridge jumps out at you: at least twenty steps to go up and down. Not much heart disease in Venice. A lot of aching bones, though, and rheumatism caused by the damp.

You're forever going up and down, even in the *calli*: Venice is never flat, it's a continuous unevenness, all lumps, bumps, hump-backed bulges, dips, dents, depressions; the *fondamente* slope to the *rii*, the *campi* are quilted with manhole covers like buttons sunk in the swellings of a sofa. This chapter is dedicated not only to legs, but to the labyrinth: or rather to the pair of corporeal labyrinths, the two snail-shells in the depths of the ears that give you your sense of balance.

I don't know how true this story is, I'm passing it on

as it was told to me: count the columns of the Doge's Palace, on the exposed side facing St Mark's Basin, opposite the island of San Giorgio. Starting at the corner, reach the fourth column; you will notice that it's slightly out of alignment with the others, a few centimetres further forwards. If you rest your back against the column and try to slip around its circumference, starting at the outside of the colonnade, you won't be able to keep from falling off the microscopic white marble step that rises from the grey stones of the shore. Try as you may, you'll lose your balance and fall from the step even if you squash yourself against the column or stretch one leg out to the side to swing around the rim and pass the critical point. As a child I was always trying to do it, it was much more than a challenge or a game, it really made me shudder: I'd been told that condemned men were given that final chance of salvation, a kind of ordeal by equilibrium, a divine judgement for acrobats; if they managed to slip around the column without setting their feet on the grey stones they would be granted mercy at the very last moment. The cruellest of illusions, which might be called *torture by hope*, like a perverse short story by a nineteenth-century French writer. At any rate, I like that idea of death as being only a few centimetres deep, rather than the usual abyss: it isn't an overblown image and it's all the more frightening for that. Perhaps dying will be like that: perhaps the step is tiny, perhaps you don't really fall into a chasm, look, it's just three centimetres deep, go on, you just need to keep your balance, it's easy...

Prepare to board a vaporetto (in Venetian, *batèo*), stand and wait on the landing stages (*imbarcadèri*): the vaporetto pulls up, giving you a jolt that takes you by surprise like a sudden slap on the back. Climb on board and, again, don't sit down, stay upright on the deck, beneath the external roof; feel with your legs the trembling of the engine in the vaporetto's belly, making your calves vibrate, the roll that constantly forces you to shift the weight of your body from one leg to the other, making you tense and relax muscles you didn't know you had. I should point out to you that on public transport, the vaporetti of the Venetian Public Transport Company (ACTV), you will pay five times as much as a Venetian resident, who can buy a special card, the Cartavenezia, at a much more modest rate.

And, please, do stand in gondolas. But take care: in this case I'm referring to the ferry gondolas, the *traghetti*. These can be found at various points along the Grand Canal: for half the price of a cup of coffee they take you from one bank to the other, at spots more or less distant from the four big bridges that cross the Canal. You'll find the gondola ferries beside the railway station, on the

right as you come out; at San Marcuola; at Rialto by the
fish market, and further off in Riva del Vin and Riva del
Carbon; at Sant'Angelo and San Tomà; at Santa Maria del
Giglio, and towards the Punta della Dogana. It isn't a
service for tourists, or rather most of the passengers are
Venetians, who use them to save time. The *traghetto*
gondolas are slightly broader than the tourist ones. They
could actually hold up to twenty passengers, plus two
gondoliers, one at the prow and one at the stern; but
local byelaws decree that the maximum permitted
number of passengers is fourteen.

On the other hand, watch out for tourist gondola
trips, which are expensive. As a general rule, if you
accept panoramic jaunts on rowing boats or motor boats,
be scrupulous about checking the rates before you climb
aboard: ask if the prices refer to the boatload as a whole
or to each individual passenger. You'll often find yourself
witnessing unpleasant arguments involving tourists who
disembark convinced that they have to pay, let's say, ten
ducats, when they're suddenly asked to fork out forty
because they got in with their consort and their two
children. In any case, remember that the public transport
of the ACTV, the vaporetti and motor boats, will take you
practically anywhere for the price of a beer or a weekly
magazine. Travel the length of the Grand Canal, and then
tour the city putting in at the Giudecca, San Giorgio, San

Clemente, San Lazzaro degli Armeni, the Lido, the cemetery at San Michele. Don't miss the little cruises on the lagoon; get on the motor boats at the Fondamente Nuove, and you'll discover parallel Venices, counter-venices, paravenices, antivenices: Murano, to which the master glassworkers were exiled seven centuries ago because their foundries were causing too many fires; psychedelic Burano, with its plasterwork as brightly coloured as a sixties album cover; Le Vignole, Mazzorbo, Torcello; Punta Sabbioni, San Francesco del Deserto, Il Cavallino, Jesolo; Pellestrina, Chioggia, Sottomarina.

The lagoon has hundreds of species of fish, amphibians and birds, it plays host to the past and the future of biology: it's a filling station for parties of migrating birds which find their way back to it by memory, and it's also a fantastical laboratory where pestilential mutant seaweeds are patented with genetic codes distorted by industrial pollution.

At one time it was more customary to move about in boats. Until eight hundred years ago there were hardly any bridges, and movable gangways were used instead. *Tòpe, sàndoli, mascaréte, s'ciopóni, peàte, puparìni, caorline, sanpieròte*: the problem today isn't getting hold of a boat – they're cheaper than cars – but finding a permanent mooring. The mooring-posts are individual, and recorded in a city register. No double parking along the *rii*!

Venice is an Anglo-Saxon city: many houses have their own front door on to the street, separate from the house next door, however tiny it might be. That used to apply even to the poorest buildings, the oldest working-class blocks, built five hundred years ago, with surprisingly modern urban planning arrangements and government finance.

Nowadays people in Venice do a lot more walking. Originally the houses and buildings lining the canals were built with their façades turned towards the water, with the main entrance facing the boat's landing stage. The secondary entrances opened on to the *calli*: the bit of Venice we mostly use today is the back; the city turns its back on us, it arses us around.

You can see this in the bridges, too: many of them are out of kilter, as though the islands had shifted, sliding in opposite directions. The bridges are built on a diagonal: the sides, whether in brick or cast iron, perform acrobatic twists. The flights of steps look like flows of hardened lava that have pushed their way along weird slopes off to the side. The odd one announces as much with its name – the Ponte Storto, or Twisted Bridge. It's because in many cases the *calli* leading to the two shores of the canal weren't aligned to meet a bridge: they were simply outlets on to the water, to board or disembark from boats, to load or unload goods. In other words, the houses came first, and between the houses the *calli*, set out according to rules of their own; the bridges were built afterwards: it was the bridges that had to adjust to the mismatch between *calli* that *almost* faced one another, but weren't perfectly aligned from one shore of the *rio* to the other.

As you probably know from pictures on the television news, you can end up getting your feet soaked as you walk around Venice: the high water, or *acqua alta*, is an unfortunate combination of bad weather, winds and currents cramming the high tide into the lagoon. It happens particularly from October to December; but a little while ago, in April, I came out of the cinema into a completely flooded *campiello*; I carried a girlfriend home on my shoulders, up to the knee in the icy water, making slow headway, for several hours: an act – literally – of chivalry that cost me three days of cold and fever.

Venetians reserve the name *braghe acqua alta* – high water breeches – for trousers that are cut too short, inelegant ankle-flappers that look as if they were cut deliberately so as not to soak the hems. *Acqua alta* is a disaster that started in the twentieth century; parts of the lagoon were filled in, deep channels were dug to keep the oil-tankers from running aground, allowing the sea to flood the city precipitously, within only a few minutes. The low, spongy islands of the lagoon, the *baréne*, brushwood-covered, eaten away by the motion of the waves, were no longer able to absorb the excess tide. The ancient Venetians diverted river-courses to keep the floods from pouring too much water into the lagoon. And Venice itself was originally called the City of the High Shore, *Civitas Rivoalti*, Rialto: although more recent archaeologists may not agree, it was said to have been born on the nucleus of islands that was raised slightly above the water level.

With less than a metre's difference in altitude, many areas are already under water; a serious emergency arises beyond one metre ten. On the terrible night of November 4th 1966, my father swam home from work.

The sirens that sounded the alarm during the air raids of the Second World War have been kept on top of the *campanili*. Now they announce sea raids, when the *acqua alta* is about to rise: they wake you at five, six in the morning. The sleepy inhabitants fix steel bulkheads to their front doors and slide little dams into the rubberised metal frames attached to their doorposts. Even the ground-floor windows facing the water-swollen canals are reinforced: more often there's really nothing to be done, the water gushes from the manhole covers, surges up through cracks in the floor, stains the furniture, drenches the walls, ruins the paintwork. Shopkeepers dash to switch on the hydraulic pumps, frantically lift the goods from their lower shelves. Years ago, after a particularly powerful *acqua alta*, I remember improvised stalls outside the shops selling off flood-damaged shoes. Special teams of dustmen come out at dawn to set up wooden gangways in the submerged *calli*. Secondary-schoolchildren wearing knee-high rubber boots – or waders covering the whole leg – give their friends, the ones wearing ordinary shoes, a lift home; boys load the sweet cargo of a pretty classmate on to their backs; they might even give ungainly piggybacks to their teachers, arms wrapped round shoulders, hands under knees: at a distance of thirty centuries they impersonate Aeneas bringing his father Anchises to safety as they fled burning Troy. If you went out in the wrong shoes, you go into the grocer's to ask for a pair of plastic shopping bags, bag up your feet and tie the handles around your ankles. Boys with wheelbarrows ferry pedestrians across puddles big as swimming-pools and deposit them on dry land, in return for a coin. Tourists love it, take snapshots, walk about barefoot with their trousers rolled up fisherman-style, and tread on invisible underwater dog-shit; there's always one who walks blissfully on, laughing his head off and generally rejoicing, unaware that he is getting dangerously close to the edge of the submerged *fondamenta*, the invisible shore beneath his feet has come to an end, but he goes on dragging his ankles under the water until he misses his step and suddenly plunges into the canal.

Years ago a lawyer friend of mine was accompanying a barrister to the court. They were walking along rickety wooden gangways, there was a gap of a metre between one and the next, and all of a sudden the barrister vanished: all that emerged from the water was the sleeve of a jacket, at the top of it a wrist with a gold watch, the hand desperately waving the leather briefcase in the air; my friend grabbed it as he passed. The barrister discussed the case in court completely drenched, dripping, smugly clutching the documents that had been saved from the water.

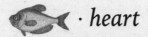 · *heart*

Do PEOPLE FALL IN LOVE more easily in Venice? According to the theologian Tadeusz Zulawskij, 'repeated tests and biochemical analyses confirm that there is no place in the world more stimulating of hormone production'. For his part, Professor Isaak Abrahamowitz, psychoanalyst, retorts that:

> the permanent state of romantic excitement, the constant erotic frenzy induced by Venice in its visitors has the paradoxical effect of diluting the sexual impulse. It is true that it keeps desire forever inflamed, but at a mild level, without sudden fluctuations. In this way the sexual impulse is communicated to every single stratum of the individual, it melts into all the limbs, it smoothly penetrates the recesses of the soul. Eros spreads like a patch of oil from the genital apparatus to the whole human being: in so doing it increases its own diffusion, while diminishing in intensity.

The 1998 world champion body-builder, Oscar Krickstein, declared in a recent interview:

> It's strange, it's as if my body performed a soft love gym with Venice, from dawn till dusk, never stopping, at moderate pace, from the tips of my hair to my toes. Really, when I come here I make love with Venice! Without realising it I have sex with this city. In the evening I don't even feel like smashing everything, it's unbelievable! In any other part of the world, every time I set foot in a gym I wreck the joint. Here, though, I'm calmer, Venice pacifies me.

The verses of the poet Costanza Fenegoni Varotti put it even more clearly:

> I shall go out ululating this evening
> I shall grope my way drooling down the *calli*,
> To devour you with my furious kisses
> Young men cropped to zero
> Such swollen, generous trousers,
> I shall skip and jump
> On the Bridge of my Sighs
> I shall pant, tongue protruding
> Dehydrated by desire:
> I shall throw wide open all the pores of my skin,
> I shall flash a thousand tiny canines
> Beneath that werewolf moon

I shall sink my teeth into your raw, bare skulls,
To slake the parched flame
Of my most secret mouths
I will suck from your bodies
As though supping coloured sodas from a stall.

What is the upshot of these fine suggestions? Let's look at the last verse of the same poem:

But I am left here thinking of you,
cruel-skulled boys,
replace my dentures in the bitter cup,
'goodnight, my dear companion
in a thousand ardent battles'
I gently doze away
oh my rough naked boys
imagining you
invaginating you
impaginating you.

The subatomic physicist Gary Fletcher, in the chapter of his autobiography entitled 'Women and me', relates an interesting incident:

Those strange, epileptic convulsions of the personality
took hold of me every time I found myself next to a pretty
girl, setting off in me endogenous nervous discharges

quantifiable within the range of 1000–1500 biovolts. A fine problem. And the only way to resolve it was to plug myself in without further ado to the unfortunate girl's – let's call it – socket. One day, however, I was invited to a conference that was being held in Italy, and I found myself visiting Venice for the first time. Venice! The city of lovers and honeymoons! The city that had driven Othello out of his mind for love! What ill-omened effects would it have on me? I admit it, I was rather worried. As soon as I set foot in Venice, to my great surprise my attacks of *voracitas sexualis rapax* mysteriously vanished away. I didn't wish to investigate the cause of this unexpected phenomenon. I packed my bags and headed back forthwith to my beloved Minneapolis.

I shall stop here, even though I could list dozens of equally authoritative testimonies. Let us return to the question with which we began. Does one fall in love more easily in Venice? Does the heart beat faster? Should you go there with your girlfriend? Do you obtain concrete results by joining forces with Venice to bamboozle a girl? Yes, without a doubt. But allow me a brief reflection on this subject, after which we shall pass straight on to more practical matters.

So: these old ploys – surrounding yourself with a splendid landscape, setting yourself off against a charming backdrop in order to perform your seduction – what do they signify? I want to make a strong impression, I present myself against a beautiful background as though my body were haloed by wonderful images: landscape becomes aura (applying the same principle, I dress nicely because clothes are a secretion of my skin).

'Here all you need to do is wrap the landscape around you,' wrote Andrea Zanzotto. Now consider this situation from the reverse perspective: it's as though the landscape were concentrated in certain nodal points: the background condenses, crystallises into a figure that is me. That's why, when things are going right, I can't help thinking: is she kissing me or the landscape? Another risk: unattractive figures stand out against a picturesque background, they're more conspicuous. So, if you don't feel like Miss Universe or Mr Hollywood, declare your love against a background of discarded rubbish, venture your first kiss surrounded by farting exhaust pipes, hold hands with your back to a stinking refinery: you will be the only beautiful thing in the landscape, an irresistible concentration of splendours, you will glitter like a gemstone in the mud. Do your seducing at Porto Marghera!

But I promised you practical advice. Is it true that in Venice people make love outdoors, on every street corner? Let's make one thing clear. Most young Venetian couples don't have cars; as you can see, even bicycles are forbidden in the city. Where are you supposed to go when your parents are at home? All teenagers have their own secret places, niches at the end of secluded *calli*, gloomy courtyards plunged in silence, and I'm certainly not going to be the one to tell you where they are. You can find them on your own (or even better, in company!), and you'll enjoy them all the more.

Certainly, everybody knows that the peeping Tom behind the chinks of the shutters never sleeps. Study the situation, take a look around: are the doorways full of doorbells? Does the lamplight glare? Are all those windows barred? What's hiding behind the corner this time? A dead end or a busy *calle*? By these stone steps descending to the *rio*, are boats passing by with their stereos up at full volume, to stop and pick you up when you least expect it? Are flotillas of gondolas with serenading musicians about to descend on you?

Choose the doorways without doorbells, which are often the entrances to shops. Exploit the corners under broken streetlights. Don't forget the freight barges docked sleepily in deserted *rii*, damp but discreet; step lightly aboard, and when you've finished, leave no signs of your passage, no contraceptive, rolled-up tissues, little hearts carved into the side with a penknife: it wouldn't be polite to someone who's shown you such hospitality. Some people take the vaporetto to the Lido at night, in the spring or the early autumn, before and after the swimming season: the beach offers the empty cabins of the bathing establishments, although this one's become much riskier over the past few years because every now and again security guards do the rounds, armed with torches.

In the historic centre, try to find a hiding place from which you can make a dignified and hastily dissembling exit at any moment, as if nothing had happened. Unless yours is an exhibitionistic, brazen love that thrives on risk: but in that case you don't need my advice, and you won't feel intimidated wherever you go.

All of these things are perfectly obvious to Venetian lovers. I went through my own stage of emotional buccaneering, between the ages of fifteen and twenty, searching for open-air hiding places in the streets. I'd like to tell you five little stories that occurred during that time: perhaps they happened to me, perhaps I was told about them, perhaps I witnessed them.

Story number one: there's a couple at the end of a *calle* leading to a canal; they're standing in the recess of a low doorway. They're both in an extremely unbuttoned state. All of a sudden a lady and a gentleman appear, accompanied by a little girl of about five years old. The gentleman is holding a map. They don't turn on their heels: the man persists, he doesn't seem to realise that he's intruding, he asks for directions. Without batting an eyelid, the embracing teenage couple, locked together from thorax to pelvis, hide their naked chests by pressing them together, while a curtain of shirts shields them from the side. As though it were the most natural thing in the world, the boy explains the way to the little family of lost tourists, the girl smiles too, and every now and again she kindly adds some extra detail to the itinerary so that husband and wife won't get lost again and don't annoy the hell out of some other unfortunate couple.

Story number two: after lengthy peregrinations, a boy and a girl finally find a fine big doorway, magnificently out of the way. They sit down on the wide, commodious monumental steps and commence an interesting exchange of opinions. Between one kiss and the next, and through half-closed lids, their dreamily sentimental eyes become aware of television cameras pointed straight at them: there are at least five of them, a multi-media shooting squad. It must be the headquarters of some major company. Meanwhile, in his lodge, the night-watchman will have been sitting, as if in a director's box, facing a wall of screens, greatly appreciating the aerial shots and side-shots, full face and profile, the televisual demonstrations of affection, the cathode-ray caresses.

Story number three: here we have another pair of lovers who don't really know where to go. Every night, at about three in the morning, on a bench in the middle of an open *campo*, you will see this kind of mobile sack. A pair of legs sticks out at the bottom, clothed from knees to feet. At the top there's a mass of restless material, a greatcoat enclosing a girlfriend squatting on the bench, hunkered over a boyfriend. They're making love: in full view of everyone, were it not for the fact that everyone is fast asleep.

Story number four: a boy and a girl are making love standing up in the niche of a barred doorway, in a twilit courtyard. The girl's back is resting against the door, the boy is pounding away at her with urgent and hearty thrusts. Awkward and uncomfortable. The boy misses a beat, slips forward, crashes into a massive sharp-edged padlock. Hurts like hell. He whispers an imprecation, and begins to swell again, but this time with pain rather than passion: a bruise right on the very tip. A metre away the shutters squeak, and a mysterious hand peeps from a ground-floor window, to set on the sill a roll of bandages and a bottle of lotion for the relief of contusions. The healing little hand discreetly withdraws.

Story number five: a girl goes home late, darting distracted glances, hang on, don't I know him? Yes, it's really him, leaning against a well-curb, right in the middle of the *campiello*. There's someone else there, kneeling in front of him. Without even thinking of interrupting the girlfriend who is busying herself with his pelvic zone, the boy returns the glance of the girl crossing the *campiello*, recognises her in turn, raises an arm in salutation, beams confidently and calls a jovial 'Hi!'.

Let's try to end with a flourish. Go back and count the columns of the Doge's Palace, still starting with the corner column, but this time on the side facing the *piazzetta*, towards the Marciana Library. When you reach the seventh column look up and read, like a comic strip, like a silent animated cartoon, the saddest and most heart-rending love story ever told. It's an octagonal *amore* that runs anti-clockwise: the first scene is the one carved on the same plane as the façade.

Side one: a boy walking along the street. A long-haired girl appears at the window.

Side two: they've arranged their first date. The boy and the girl converse charmingly.

Side three: the girl strokes his forehead.

Side four: they kiss.

Side five: they make love.

Side six: a baby is born. Mother and father cuddle it in swaddling clothes.

Side seven: the baby has grown.

Side eight: the child is dead. The parents weep, lying on the grave.

There are three things that I would like to point out

about this tear-jerking story. The first is that even in the Middle Ages girls took the initiative by extending a hand. The second is that even in the Middle Ages people went to bed together before they got married. The third is that everything happens in a vertical plane. The characters are always arranged symmetrically, their gestures mirrored, bundled in tunics and robes that fall plumb: but not in the fifth frame. Beneath the sheets, crumpled waves of fabric, in a drapery of marine folds, swept away by the linen storm, the two lovers lie on a kind of lozenge, a slanting rectangle: the bed, which has moved slantwise, the mattress rhomboidal. It was passion that carried the bed around the room, that sent it rolling and bouncing slowly across the floor. Love is diagonal: it upsets aesthetic canons, routs the rigid choreographies of a gothic bas-relief.

 · *hands*

YOU SPONTANEOUSLY FEEL LIKE touching it. You brush it with your fingers, caress it, pat it, pinch it, feel it. You put your hands on Venice.

You lean on the parapets of the bridges. The balustrades of the Rialto Bridge have been polished by millions of hands: a sign that you, too, are taking a few molecules of stone away with you. It stays caught in your pores, trapped in the ridges of your fingerprints.

You run your hands over the blank-rubbed metal poles next to the canals.

You stretch out your arms and touch both sides of a *calle*, from one side to the other. In the narrower ones you can't even elbow your way through. They seem to be made to measure for your shoulders: you almost find yourself walking down them sideways. I can point you to one behind Campo San Polo: it's actually called Calle

Stretta, or Narrow Calle, 65 centimetres wide.

You scratch the crumbling plaster, the cracked and corroded bricks. That's where treasure-hunt organisers hide their clues. And where dealers hide their baggies.

You lift an arm and touch the roof of the *sottoportico*, the covered passageway. At Dorsoduro, coming down from the Ponte del Vinante, you can easily touch the plaster above the entrance. Chewing gum of every flavour and colour has been stuck there: old mineralised liquorice gum, yellowish and seemingly tobacco-stained, next to shocking-pink fluorescent strawberry and bright green peppermint Chernobylian sapphires, in a mosaic of hardened rubber tesserae. In the summer of 1993 I set myself the task of counting them, and there were 897. Four years later there are 3,128. One would imagine that the monument authorities would clamp down on this impressive abstract tessellation, the collective handiwork – jawwork, more properly – of those masticating master mosaicists.

You refresh yourself with water from the drinking fountains. You block the tip and send three-metre geysers gushing from the spout.

You stroke affectionate cats.

You're tempted to test the consistency of the ropes of the vaporetti, which groan as they stretch, tied to the docking jetties, but the sailor on board gestures to you to keep away. They could slice your wrist right through: he himself handles them with a pair of tough leather gloves.

You settle for clutching the strange metal mushrooms on the sides of the vaporetti, the bits that the rope is wrapped around, and their giant relatives on the Riva dei Sette Martiri in St Mark's Basin, the stone cylinders on the Zattere. On the *fondamente*, curiosity aroused, you lift heavy rings hooked to the ground, set into the paving stones: they're for mooring the boats.

You grip the forearms of the gondoliers when they help you to board the *traghetti*. For safety's sake you also hold on to the mooring posts planted in the water, the *brìcole**.

You run your fingers over the rowlocks of the gondolas, the ones that stand out at the stern, the *fórcole*. The Futurist artist Boccioni invented nothing: his *Unique Forms in the Continuity of Space* is a statue that shows a body in movement, but looks like an assemblage of *forcole*. A man walks, scattering volumes of muscle into the space, forgetting that they are inside him. He wears the movement, a body increased by volume, like superimposed slides of a walk, a sequence of steps fixed one inside the other, persisting in the retina. That statue suggests to you that the *forcola* is also a thing both fixed

---

*Bricola in Italian, *brìcola* in Venetian; similarly *forcola/fórcola*, below.

and mobile: movement told from the perspective of stillness. We should really put them all to the test like that, all the statues in the world, by putting them in gondola sterns to see how the oar rests on them, to discover all of art's directions.

The *forcola* is anachronistic, not in the sense of being old-fashioned, quite the reverse: it's a futuristic object projected into the past. It looks as though it was dreamed up by a twentieth-century Finnish designer who climbed into a time machine and fixed it on to the gondola hundreds of years in advance. When was Alvar Aalto born? In the sixteenth century?

Now observe how the oar touches it: with its handles, elbows, opened rings, the *forcola* allows a dozen angles, rests, furcations. In any other boat in the world, a single oarsman, with a single oar, on one side only, would end up turning comically in circles. On a gondola, thanks to the boat's asymmetrical centre of gravity, it darts straight ahead, switches into reverse, slows and accelerates, brakes, halts, heads off diagonally, turns a right angle, keeps balance, deadens the waves. The oar spoons the water, spanks it, scoops it, digs it, cuts it, kneads it, tickles it, turns it like a ladle, forces it like a crowbar. The oar dives suddenly, re-emerges floating almost horizontally at water level, but if necessary it plunges vertically, in a few free square centimetres, with a flick of the wrist it twists like a screwdriver, elegantly disengaging the twelve-metre black wooden beast from an impossible jam.

You go and see the gondolas leaving their main parking place, in the Orseolo Basin, beside St Mark's Square. They inch away, dozens at a time, without touching each other, the gondoliers chattering among them as they row, greeting one another, calling out to each other, paying no heed to the low bridge their noses are about to crash into: at the last minute, almost without looking, they bend their necks, brush the arch's underside, comb their hair on the brick vault.

The gondoliers row with one leg in front and one behind, the hindmost foot resting on a tiny raised wedge: the energy pivots first on the heel, then the sole, then the toes. Observe their bodies at rest, vaguely pithecan-thropic: arms dangling slightly forwards, shoulders round, the back of the neck, the shoulder blades, the big collarbones. From the left hand to the right they are surrounded by a U of upper-case muscles.

You go back and spread your arms around the circumference of the well-curbs, closed with bronze covers. If you fancy yourself as a percussionist, you go and play on the well-curb in San Silvestro: it echoes like a West Indian steel drum. Every square inch has a different note, deep, mute, clear, faint.

Little drummers below the age of twelve go charging about the streets on November 11th, St Martin's Day. They run into the shops, ring the bell and go on hitting saucepans with wooden spoons until they're given sweets and coins as a reward. They sing a nursery rhyme sung to the tune of the anthem of the *bersaglieri*:

San Martìn xe 'ndà in sofìta
a trovar la so' novìssa
so' novìssa no ghe gera
san Martìn col culo par tèra!

St Martin went to the attic to find his betrothed, his betrothed wasn't there, St Martin ended up on the ground on his backside. What does this little song tell us? It tells us that even the saints have an intense emotional life; that the eternal feminine urges us upwards, into the attic, because love is a human being surrounded by sky; because without your girlfriend you are fated to plunge back into incestuous contact with mother earth. And naturally all these things are sung to us by children, little *amori*, who alone know the secret of sex because, as everyone knows but no one can bring themselves to admit, they are sexuality, they are Eros. Once I even met a gang of twenty-five of my friends wandering the streets bashing pans and singing the 'San

Martìn': they were all unemployed, and actually managed to scrape a little extra money together.

You close your eyes and read the physiognomies of the statues, the bas-reliefs, the fluted mouldings, the alphabets carved in the stones at head-height. Venice is an uninterrupted Braille handrail.

 · *face*

VÓLTO IN VENETIAN MEANS a mask, like *persona* in Latin. Anthropological studies of Carnival will tell you that between Epiphany and Lent the world used to turn upside down. The son lost respect for his father, people changed sex, it was no longer forbidden to mock the king. All of this served to confirm the order of the universe. To infringe the law was to celebrate it. Violating it once only, during a compulsory feast, meant acknowledging its dominion the rest of the time.

In Venice you walk around wearing your own face, taking it for what it really is: a public place. This is a city where privacy doesn't exist. You are constantly meeting people, you greet them seven times a day, you go on talking as you part, until you're twenty metres away from each other, raising your voice as you disappear into the crowd. Your neighbours' faces are on the other side of the *calle*: a metre away. It's very difficult to do things in secret, to have a life of your own, to hide your own visits, your affairs, your adulteries.

If you live here you sometimes feel the desire to go for a liberating walk, leaving yourself at home, taking a stroll to have a little break from your personality. You abandon your thoughts, you forget yourself. You go out and do nothing but look around, you wish it was the landscape that was thinking rather than you, showing you a series of spectacles to contemplate, sounds, smells, scenes to acknowledge and nothing more: but then all of a sudden, somebody's greeting you, calling you by name, restoring you to yourself, you remember who you are.

Henry James wrote in a novella that Venice is like an interior, an apartment consisting of corridors and drawing-rooms: you're always walking inside it, you're never really outside it, the outside doesn't exist even in the street. Apparently (which is to say: maskedly) the Venetian passion for the mask was born from this need to be incognito, to protect your own identity. Because this is a city where public life forces you to drag your character on to the surface of your skin, to transfer it permanently from your soul to your face. You too become a character, vaguely puppet-like, a stylised form of yourself.

Harlequin, Pantaloon, Colombine are street types,

drained of themselves as though tattooed from head to toe with their own physiognomies. They live on the surface of their own bodies. Their bodies proclaim their every intention. There is no false bottom, no second layer. They act without reserve, their reactions are exaggerated: appetite is ravenous hunger (Harlequin); ambition naked avarice (Pantaloon); love sugary sentimentality (Colombine). There is no filter between movement and action. These figures behave comically, they make you laugh, they seem superficial, but they aren't really: they are impersonations of what happens to nature when it is forced to leave its own recesses, to migrate to the surface and live there always. Each of them is a set of expressive gesticulations, a bundle of ways of saying and doing quarrelsome things, of relating to other people. Their masks are not a double face, a supplementary identity or, worse, a phoney piece of play-acting: they are condensations of the face, *hardened faces*. By dint of rubbing against their public role, their skin has been tanned as hard as leather. What happens to the soul when it is fixed to the skin and exiled to the face, when it is forced to express itself at all times? The commedia dell'arte and Goldoni's masked comedies aren't farces, they're surface tragedies.

Amongst the many traditional masks used during the Carnival I would like to mention only one, a female mask that expresses a rather horrible attitude towards women: the *moréta* is a black oval with holes only over the eyes. It was held on without straps, you had to bite a kind of grip, an inward-facing mouth-height protrusion. Women who wore it were forced to be silent.

A micro-mask, likewise female, was the fake mole, called the little fly, *moschéta*, used not to conceal, but to emphasise a point in the face or the neck, as though the flesh had been scalded, burnt by the concentration of gazes through the lens of desire.

There are huge numbers of mask shops, all varying in price and quality. The papier mâché ones are the most expensive, it takes time and skill to make them, and they are the only ones made according to the traditional method. If you put on masks of other materials, pressed cardboard, china, terracotta – yes, they make them with terracotta, too! – bear in mind that they are very fragile, actually unusable, except to be hung on the wall.

What is the world capital of Carnival? Rio, Viareggio, Venice? And what parties must on no account be missed in the lagoon between Maundy Thursday and Shrove Tuesday? Relax, stop feeling you're always in the wrong place at the wrong time. Now I'm going to tell you where to go, and how to gatecrash the right bash. Go out of your house, in your own city, on any ordinary day. That's where the party is! The processions invade the streets at all hours: look at the costumes made of sheet metal, headlights and tyres, the chassis camouflaging the whole body, not just the face, wrapping up the whole of the appearance, standing in for the face. The carnival spirit is rooted within the urban population, in that everyone has his own fashion-parade car-costume, his own carnival music booming from his car stereo, everyone takes part in the merry-making with horn trumpets and exhaust-pipe explosions. They launch into a language of drunken gestures, insult each other from one lane to another, curse each other's family trees, unite in raging against the white-gloved master of ceremonies with his little whistle: prohibitions are violated, transgression rules, the universe is turned upside down. In Venice the Carnival isn't much, it lasts a few weeks give or take: the whole of the rest of the world is in disguise from the first of January to the thirty-first of December.

There isn't a trace of a car, not here. Rich and poor get around on foot, they don't flaunt their income with wheeled displays. Are the streets of Venice democratic? Or do they mask true social inequalities? Both things are true. But if the mood takes you, for a few hours you can pass yourself off as a great lord, without having to hire a limousine. It's easier to trick and seduce, two words that mean the same thing. Venice, the ideal city for budding Casanovas.

 · *ears*

YOU HAVE TO GET USED TO silence and noise. You pass suddenly from the muffled courtyards to the Grand Canal, honking with boats, from the solitary gondola to the fleet of serenades, with the accordion and the tourists clapping along and the big fat baritone with the well-oiled, well-ombra'd voice. The gondoliers have a portable klaxon in their throats: a gondola doesn't make a sound, so when they're about to turn at right angles they give a warning shout: 'Òe, pòpe!': the 'pòpe' doesn't refer to the pontiff, it's the rowing space behind the stern. There are convex mirrors to avoid collisions, and roadsigns showing speed limits for motor boats. They look as if they've come from another automotive age: in the Grand Canal the maximum permitted speed is 5 km/h, in the Giudecca Canal it's 11 km/h, in St Mark's Basin it's 20 km/h. Policemen, taxi drivers and funeral services thunder about in motor boats. If you're curious to see the red nozzles of the floating fire engines with their water-firing tubes fixed to the side, you'll find them moored beneath the arches of the central fire station, at Ca' Foscari.

Foghorns enlarge the far-off ships, expanding the port through the air.

The depredations of the cats wake you up at night. They challenge one another to duels, hissing in each other's faces, yowling oestrous miaows. The cats cat, the dogs dog and the mice mouse: at about one o'clock in the morning, the sewer rats come out into the streets to tear holes in the plastic rubbish bags that have been left outside, then dive into the canals and swim across them to reach the piles of garbage on the other side. *Pantegana*, the Italian word for a sewer rat, derives from *mus ponticus*, sea rat from the Pontus: oriental rats, in the Middle Ages they brought the black plague from the Black Sea, hidden in the bites of their fleas on galleys loaded with merchandise. The Chiesa del Redentore on the Giudecca and the Madonna della Salute are both temples to the defeat of the pestiferous creatures, monuments to deratification.

You walk around with the poems of Pascoli to listen live to his phonetic transcriptions of the language of the birds. Monovocalic turtle doves have learned only the vowel *u*, they greet one another by name, they're all called Turturu. Blackcaps, blackbirds, swallows, starlings, nightingales, unidentified chirping objects, nests of ocarinas, boughs blossoming with pipes, referees' whistles on legs.

The take-off of the pigeons whirls like the ignition of a broken-winded engine, a gear failing to engage. The sparrows silently steal your crisps as you enjoy an outdoor aperitif.

In the summer the electric microsaws of the cicadas act as spies, informing headquarters about the gardens hidden among the houses. The secret services have scattered them about the place like electronic bugs dropped from helicopters.

The gulls wheel screeching above the market stalls of Santa Margherita, the fishmongers throw flying fish through the air, feather-light sardines, silver fish against the blue sky: the gulls swallow them mid-flight. They follow you alongside the motor boats, motionless, suspended a metre from your hand, flying at the same speed as the boat, waiting for you to throw them a snack.

In the lagoon there are invisible streets in the middle of the water. These are the navigable canals, the ones with the deeper bottoms; double rows of trunks mark the way for the boats so that they don't get stuck in the shallows. The gulls rest on the tops of these trunks, each on his little studio apartment a few centimetres square. They snooze on the *bricole* of the *rii*. They all wake up at the same time, arranging to meet the little old ladies who scatter crumbs and crusts on the Zattere.

The little bubbles of the crabs burst on the surface of the canals. The stagnant water shivers for a moment, its deep sleep disturbed by the tail of a sea bass, a grey mullet's fin.

Choose your heraldic symbol, the resonant coat of arms of your line: Venice is a totemic city, inhabited by thousands of allegories in flesh and blood, skin, feathers, flippers, symbolic bestiaries, living animals more chimerical than the stone-carved lions.

Go down the Rialto Bridge on the side of the market. Close your eyes as you walk: listen to the Babel of languages spoken by tourists from all over the world, concentrated along fifty metres of *calle*.

A blind writer said that for him a fine day is a day of wind, a day of rain. You can hear the trees crumpling the air in the background. The density of the pelting rain, its impact with objects, allows you to guess the shape of the city: here there's a very tall *palazzo*, over there the awning of a bar.

In Venice the same cloud drops slanting bucketloads on a *campo*, but hits the narrow *calli* with well-aimed arrows of rain: the drops suddenly ease away, and yet this gutter floods, the canal beyond is covered with little circles, as though a billion anglers were casting off at the same moment. With a bit of practice you can recognise the sound of the most impalpable rain, you will hear the lightest cloud, the drops bouncing at ground level, you can listen to the fog.

The heels that echo as you walk the *calli* at night are the punctuation of your solitude.

Your day is sliced into hours and half-hours by the peals of the bells. At midnight the mother of all bells booms out: the *marangona* of St Mark's campanile commands silence.

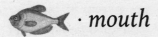 · *mouth*

IN THE MORNING you go and have breakfast on the Zattere, the city's central shore. Or facing it, on the Giudecca shore on the other side of the canal.

You return to the Zattere in the afternoon to take the sun and have an ice cream. *Gianduiotto* sounds like a chocolate from Turin, but it's eaten in Venice: an ingot of *gianduia*, chocolate and hazelnut ice cream, drowned in a glass of whipped cream.

But the true flavour of Venice isn't sweetness. If you want to test its character, you must go into a *bàcaro*, a kind of inn. They are fewer and fewer in number these days. You'll find the highest concentration of them in the *calli* near the Rialto market. I'm not going to tell you what they're called because I've decided that in this book I'm not going to name a single hotel, restaurant, bar or shop. Partly out of impartiality, partly because we

Venetians jealously guard our secrets, we don't like to give away those few places that the tourists haven't yet discovered. So take it as a challenge, a treasure hunt.

To earn the flavours of Venice, you must be capable of biting mouthfuls of the alphabet, rolling the sounds on your tongue, chewing on its dialect. If you speak any Italian at all, there's one Venetian word you use already, many times a day: *ciao*, abbreviation of *s'ciavo*, your slave. Note in passing that Italian shilly-shallies over the sound of this encounter of consonants, *s* and *c*, it has to be written with an apostrophe, *s'ciavo*. Another word of Venetian origin that's travelled around the world is *ghetto*: it derives from *getto, gettare*, to cast, because on the island reserved five centuries ago for the Jewish community there was a working foundry. Having only a limited space at their disposal, the Jews were forced to expand in a vertical direction: the houses of the Ghetto, in Cannaregio, reach the seventh and eighth floors, real skyscrapers of the day.

Try to camouflage yourself as a Venetian, or rather as a landlubbing Veneto-dweller, because I can guarantee that you won't be able to pronounce perfectly the phrase I'm about to suggest to you. When you're at the Rialto, at one end of the bridge or the other, ask the people around you: *capo, ghe xé un bàcaro qua vissìn?* ('Is there an inn nearby, messire?'). Bear in mind: the *e* in *xé* is a closed *e*. As to the infamous *x*, it's a traditional but questionable transcription of a simple Northern Italian *s* (voiced alveo-dental fricative consonant): the one in the Italian word *rosa*, just so we know where we are. After you have hissed this question, the passer-by will look at you with mild alarm before the penny drops: assessing your curious inflection, he will ask you whether by chance you have spent a few days in Rovigo, or Belluno, or Verona.

The windows of the *bàcari* offer you halved boiled eggs, rolled anchovies, crabs' claws, olives all'Ascolana, rice *arancini*, *polpettini*, stewed *saltimbocca*, *nervetti* (pork or beef tendon), fried sardines, *masanéte* (small crabs), *folpi* (small octopus), creamed cod, onions, *coppa di toro* (bull salami), wild boar ham, squares of mortadella, cubes of dressed mozzarella, parallelepipeds of gorgonzola. These are all, of course, washed down with an *ombra*, a glass of wine that was once tapped straight from the barrel behind the bar.

It isn't clear where the 'technical term' *ombra* (shadow) comes from: and that's as it should be, even its etymology should remain in darkness. At the most banal level, *ombra* might designate the misty translucency of the wine. But it's more likely that it refers to the open-air wine stalls in the summer, in the shade of the *campanili*, where people sheltered from the heat by drinking a glass of chilled wine. '*Andiamo a prendere un'ombra* – Let's go and take the shade,' was a kind of wink, implying: 'Let's go where the drinking's done.'

These delicacies in the *bàcaro* are lavish antipasti which, as you will see, are soon transformed into substitute meals, consumed standing up at the bar: one *cichéto* attracts the next, one delicious mouthful begins to compile the whole anthology of flavours.

On the other hand, you will no longer find the fried fish shops that used to exist: the *fritolìn* used to spill out into the crowded *calli*, selling blue fish, *anguelle* (eels), *marsióni* (goby), *mòi* (poor cod), cuttlefish, squid, *schìe* (shrimp). The oil soaked into the absorbent paper bags: huge slices of white or yellow polenta were cut: that was an afternoon snack, after the cinema or the football. Those with a sweet tooth, on the other hand, opted for *gardo*, pancakes made with chestnut flour, and oven-baked pears, which could also be bought in the street.

Dinner time is approaching. As an aperitif, have the barman mix you a *spriz*: soda water, white wine and, to taste, a bitter like Campari, Aperol or Select, with a slice of lemon or an olive. The *spriz* is a legacy of the Hapsburg occupation and, from here to Trieste, according to which bar you go into, you'll find it mixed in a hundred different ways, as if following the changing dialects. It goes down very nicely, without a kick; it seems light enough, but it'll take you by surprise on an empty stomach.

Ready to take a risk? OK, even in Venice fast food outlets are springing up all over the place, but I'd like to suggest three dishes in particular. Perhaps to be tried on different occasions, because they have demanding flavours. You could flabbergast your taste buds and startle your paramours: the high onion content is a foolproof anti-kiss device.

Dish number one: *bìgoli in salsa*. The *bìgoli* are thick wholemeal spaghetti, the sauce is a sautéed, salty mixture of onions and sardines.

A phonetic digression. Given that I've already let you try out their name, this time I'll also have to describe the method of masticating the sound. *Bìgolo* is the singular, but the *l* isn't sounded, the tip of the tongue stays down, it doesn't actually rise to touch the upper alveolar ridge, as in a normal *l*. The back part of the tongue arches, hinting at the soft fantasy of an *e*: 'bigo(e)o', and you just have to separate the two Siamese *o*'s. In the plural, these subtleties disappear, because the vowels are different, the *l* is written down, *bìgoli*, but you don't actually pronounce it: 'bìgoi'. The same thing with the words you've come across in earlier chapters. Forco*l*a, 'fórco(e)a', plural forco*l*e, 'fórcoe'. Brico*l*a, 'brìco(e)a', plural brico*l*e, 'brìcoe'. Cu*l*o, 'cu(e)o', plural cu*l*i, 'cui'...

Dish number two: *sarde in saór*. These are fried sardines, left to marinate for a day in a sautéed mixture of onions, with wine and vinegar: and that is the *saór*, the *sapore*, or flavour. Served cold, they are the main dish of the feast of the Redentore, on the third Sunday in July: they are eaten in boats, swaying in St Mark's Basin, or on tables carried down from home to the *fondamenta*, before the fireworks begin. In winter the calories are increased by adding pine nuts and raisins to the *saór*.

Dish number three: *figà a la venessiana*. Calves' liver is cooked neither too much nor too little in the obligatory sautéed onions. Some people add a glass of red wine or Marsala to the pan.

Late in the evening you can drink in company in Campo Santa Margherita, the summer centre of Venice's post-prandial nightlife. The winter equivalent is in Cannaregio, on the Fondamenta della Misericordia.

 · *nose*

E ACH *RIO* HAS ITS OWN PERSON-
ALITY. Some are very expansive, they
enwrap you immediately in their chronic stench. The
most pungent are the Rio delle Muneghéte on the border
between the *sestieri* of Santa Croce and San Polo, and the
fetid bend between the Fondamenta del Remedio and the
Sotopòrtego della Stua, behind the Querini Stampalia
Foundation. Others have a more introverted, false
character: only total low tide, parched dryness, reveals
their feculent nature, which spills inexorably along the
pipes and exhales from the discharges of sinks and bidets
at the lowest levels. Some years ago work began on the
excavation of the *rii*, to remove the muddy black bottom.
At the 1997 Biennale, the American artist Mark Dion
sieved all the objects buried in about ten cubic metres of
intractable lagoon mud: he catalogued hundreds of
fragments of china, flooded lamps, bottles without a

message, shipwrecked dolls, amphibious tyres, washing machines and heaters that might have belonged to Captain Nemo.

Our grandparents were happy to swim in St Mark's Basin in the summer. But some people suggest that the water wasn't all that clean even then: perhaps they had different standards of hygiene in those days. As a child, returning from the Lido in a vaporetto after a day at the beach, I would see the little boys of Castello throwing themselves into the water, diving head-first from the tops of the widest *bricole*: but if I had been born two centuries ago, in the evening, from the Rialto Bridge, I would have caught sight of Lord Byron taking a dip in the Grand Canal. On the morning of January 1st, intrepid seventy-year-old *'ibernisti'* plunge into the freezing sea off the Lido in front of the cameras, to bring an icy frisson to the New Year's Day television news.

Many houses empty the water from their sinks and basins, and perhaps other things besides, into the *rii*. Not for nothing does an old Venetian proverb say – no, first I'll refer you to the translation of the translation, setting out its moral significance in advance. The meaning of the proverb is more or less this: there are historical periods in which even good-for-nothings manage to accomplish certain things. And, vice versa, demonstrating skill in some service or other is not the same as excelling at it, because in some situations anybody at all can achieve a good result. Here is the proverb: *d'istà, anca i stronsi gaégia.* Translation: in the summer, even turds float. How did this maxim come about? One July afternoon, some nameless Venetian philosopher must have taken a stroll along the shore of a canal, and stopped to stare thoughtfully at a long regatta of floating shit. Five minutes will have been enough. Not like his Chinese colleague sitting on the river-bank for years waiting for the corpse of his enemy to pass by!

Another sublime aesthetic precept reads as follows: if you want to laugh, you must talk about shit. *Se se vol ridar, bisogna discórar de merda.* A grandiose vision of the comic, which makes up in abundance for the loss of the second part of Aristotle's *Poetics*, the one dedicated to comedy. But now I want to challenge this proverb: it doesn't say that talking about shit necessarily makes people laugh. I'll tell you a story in which excrement provokes not crass sniggers but sympathy and human tenderness. It's a titanic undertaking, I realise. So I turn for inspiration to the muse of alphabetic crap, the god of the metabolism of the narrative body, should he exist. And yes, now that I come to think of it he does, he's Niccolò Tommaseo: his crusty statue in the Campo Stefano rests its backside on a pile of bound volumes, and from beneath his coat-tails there spills a diarrhetic discharge of tomes and manuscripts. The Venetians have nicknamed him *il Cagalibri*, the Book-Shitter.

Refine my words, O Niccolò: let me offend neither nostrils nor pupils, let me sully neither pristine page nor sheet of toilet roll.

I can begin my story.

In the eighties, groups of tourists from Eastern Europe started coming to Venice. Dressed to the nines, shirts and jackets of inflammable acrylic; men in slippers, women wearing the kind of pale eye-shadow that in Italy you generally find as a free gift in bags of crisps. From dawn till dusk they wandered along the *calli* in well-behaved committees, silent, almost stunned. They had travelled through the night from Budapest or Prague to feast their eyes on as many cities as possible in twelve hours. You could see them on the shore near the Lion Pillar of St Mark's, beside the Doge's Palace, sitting soaking their feet in the gorgonzolic water of the Basin, brackish steam sputtering from their scorching heels as they made contact with the emerald mud: they improvised refreshing footbaths, or rather water-baths, since they contributed to the purification of the waters of the Basin by carrying away a healthy dose of lagoon bacteria beneath their toenails. In the evening they set exhaustedly off again, boarding the coaches parked on the Tronchetto, close to Piazzale Roma, the car terminal at the end of the lagoon bridge.

But here is what I saw.

The scene takes place mid-morning, beneath the June sun, on the wooden gangway leading to the vaporetto mooring jetty at San Tomà, on the Grand Canal. I notice that next to the ticket office a fair-haired girl is hanging back from the rest of the group, and crouching in the corner. Her expression is pleading, her face embarrassed. She is clutching her belly with both hands. Just beside her, a woman in her fifties is trying to screen her with her body. She might be the girl's mother: she is picking sheets of newspaper out of a nearby rubbish bin, folding them out and spreading them on the ground. We all understand immediately, and turn our heads away even before the girl squats down.

End of story.

I shall say no more: because it's right to stop here, and because I was one of those who averted their heads. This is the detail I wanted to get to: those hundred pairs of eyes that forbade themselves to spy. I would call it a paradox of indifference. It's the only instance I can think of in which pretending nothing is going on was an act of solidarity; in which taking no interest in the fate of others was a demonstration of human pity.

Bear in mind that you reach the jetty of San Tomà

after three or four rather complicated twists and turns, bars and public places with emergency lavatories are thin on the ground. Imagine a foreigner who has just arrived in the city, a girl who is probably leaving the borders of her own nation for the first time in her life, after the fall of the Wall. All of a sudden she has an intestinal attack in broad daylight: on this side the city, on the other the Grand Canal with the boats and crowded vaporetti passing only a few metres away; over her head, the sun. Where can she go? She knows very well that she won't find a toilet in time; she's obliged to relieve herself before the eyes of all and sundry. But for once the eyes of all and sundry extend a hand, or rather an eyelid, of charity.

Thank you, Book-Shitter.

Let's open the windows now, and take a breath of air. So far we've been infected by foul extrusions: let's give our nostrils a bit of relief with a scented paragraph. Off to the Rialto market, from the entrance to Campo San Giacometo to the Campiello de le Becariè; not the other way around: there's a point to this trajectory. You begin by sniffing vegetables and fruit, from the *calli* beyond the Ruga Rialto, along the Grand Canal, and already your retina is painted with the colours of the vegetable pyramids, your tympanum titillated by the crackling of the polyethylene shopping baskets, the dialect cries of the fruit-vendors. But then you end your stroll at the fish market: well, yes, the aromatic parenthesis is over already, there are other malodorous paragraphs awaiting us, you'll have to get your olfactory sense accustomed to it by dulling it with fish. Cascades of viscid biomass quiver in the metal boxes, staining the crushed ice with organic grenadine. Wearing rubber boots, the fishmongers lean on their stalls, plunging their arms up to the elbow in the cool, cadaverous jelly; on their scales they fill waterproof paper bags, or clear plastic ones, using their black and blue hands, nails encrusted with black sepia, salt blood, mucilaginous slobber.

Old stone tablets set out the minimum measurements permitted for the sale of fish. You can read them at Rialto, but also in Castello near Via Garibaldi, and in Campo San Pantalón. I shall transcribe the one in Campo Santa Margherita:

RED MULLET, GREY MULLET, SARDINE,
ANCHOVY   Cent. 7

SEA BASS, GILTHEAD, DENTICE, UMBRINE,
WHITE SEA BREAM, GREY MULLET, THICK-LIPPED
GREY MULLET, BRILL, GOLDEN GREY MULLET,
FLATHEAD MULLET, LEAPING MULLET, HAKE,
SOLE, FLOUNDER, TURBOT   Cent. 12

EEL	Cent. 25
OYSTER	Cent. 5
MUSSEL	Cent. 3

In many of the *calli* you'll find old plastic bottles full of tap water on the ground resting against the walls. These are put out at night, at the foot of the shutters or against the doorposts, although some are fixed permanently with wire to outdoor gas tubes or even to hooks fixed in the plaster. They look like little milestones, marker bottles celebrating clean water: in fact they are anti-pee devices. Apparently cats give them a wide berth, can't help it, they just can't go when there's a transparent container full of water in the vicinity: I don't know which feline ethologist discovered this little trick. The fact remains that shopkeepers, businesspeople and ordinary inhabitants mark their own territory by recycling plastic bottles in this way, competing with cat-sprays, drawing up the boundaries of their own odourless map, doing battle with the olfactory geopolitics of marauding cats.

But even among humans there are some who mistake the *calli* for open-air toilets. In some hidden corners you will notice mysterious protrusions in stone, in bare or plastered brick, or cast iron. Let's start by describing them. Position: at the right-angled entrances to the *calli*, jutting from the walls, but they can also be found at the top of a bridge, leading on to Campiello San Rocco. Height: just over a metre. Shape: the stone slabs look like the triangle of a sloping roof, the brick ones a quarter of a rounded dwarf dome, a slice of focaccia, a big piece of panettone. The ones made of cast iron have potbellied protrusions and menacing, lanceolate points. What are they for? To deter human beings from peeing. The pointed metal is self-explanatory. The working of the roofed and domed reliefs is more ingenious: these are designed to send the splashes flying back against the uncouth urinator, and most importantly to pour back his own rivulets of piss on to his feet. In many cases these anti-pissoirs don't reach as far as the paving stones, the lower edge usually hanging about thirty centimetres from the ground.

The large number of these anti-toilets demonstrates one thing above all: with this kind of architectural footnote, annotations to its urban furnishings, comments in microbuilding form, Venice is obliged to assert that it is not a toilet, to deny its latrinal qualities, to contest its lavatorial status. A clear indication, then, that the unconquerable impulse inspired by the city in the devout visitor must be that of happily pissing on it.

As children we didn't know that these were ancient

anti-bogs, inverted Duchampian urinals: we played on them with miniature footballers, sending the figures sliding down them one at a time, catching each other's as they fell one on top of the other. It had a name, this game: *scainèa*, 'scalinella', or little staircase, referring to the figure's dive from these slanting slides.

A treatise could be written on Venetian street games.

Massa e pìndolo, a form of tip-cat, a kind of *campiello* cricket or baseball. Instead of a ball, there's a little wooden cylinder in the shape of a pencil sharpened at both ends: the *pìndolo*, skilfully struck with the bat on one of its two conical extremities, rose a metre from the ground, and in that brief moment, as it spun through the air, you had to strike it a second time, sending it flying as far as possible. Sometimes it hit you at full force, right in the forehead. The point-counting system was rather complicated, based on a highly entertaining game of bets taken before the shot, and on the laborious measurements of the *pìndolo* from home base, the *gècola*.

Tacco was played with heels (*tacchi*) bought from the cobbler or, in a more modern version, with silly-looking hard disk-shaped rubber tiles, simulating bowls in a two-dimensional phantom universe, a bowling flatland. But there was no jack in *tacco*, players chased after each other throwing their own heel as close as possible to their adversary's. With a well-practised flick of the wrist the heel whirled through the air, glided, landed flat.

The chalk-traced race tracks for bottle-tops, *cìmbani*: sometimes the paving stones weren't enough for us so we used to shove our bottle-tops with our fingers into the milkman's shop for great stretches of an imaginary Giro d'Italia, exotic rallies amidst the customers' feet.

And then there were *s'cioco e spana*. *Campana*. *Piera alta*.

Our peashooters were about half a metre long. The tubes of milled plastic could be bought in pet shops: they were really supposed to serve as a little supporting beam for the feet of canaries and budgerigars, trapped between the bars of their cages. The projectiles, little balls of bread dough, or carpenters' red putty: on the road sign of the Rio de la Toletta you can still see some of these, they've been stuck there for decades, like relics of an ancient shooting match. Bigger peashooters fired *canòti*, cones of rolled-up paper.

Certainly, the catalogue is far from complete: but when I was little I played the ones I've mentioned. At any rate, I think I'm part of the last generation to have learned the rules – too complicated to explain in detail. Street games have undergone a technological mutation: peashooters have made way for hydraulic water pistols, with powerful jets of five or ten metres, and with more and more devastating calibres. Children fill them at the fountain, loading them with litres of water, the ammunition tanks are becoming increasingly capacious: Liquidator 200, 500, 1000. In the seventies the children started imitating the sports of the grown-ups: a basketball basket hanging from a grating; in some less frequented *calli*, a tennis court marked out with chalk and a long piece of elastic in place of the net: endless arguments because the ball had passed over, no, under!, no, over! The arrival of the Frisbee marked the definitive, partly symbolic, plasticated industrialisation of the diminutive street gangs.

But why am I talking to you about children's games in a chapter dedicated to the nose? Because they have disappeared, leaving only their ghost, their spirit. And you smell ghosts with your nose. Spirits are breathed in and out.

Venice is crammed full of ghosts. Writers and directors have smelt them everywhere. Walking through the *calli*, they have been attacked by the demons of Malebolge, and then Madonna Lisetta, Othello, Lunardo, Countess Livia Serpieri, Miss Bordereau, Gustav von Aschenbach, Andreas von Ferschengelder, Mary and Colin. The list goes on. Let me give you an example: at San Barnabà, Katharine Hepburn fell into the canal in the film *Summertime*, and in *Indiana Jones and the Last Crusade*, Harrison Ford jumped out of a manhole cover dug specially in the same place; note that I'm talking about a secondary *campo* here, not St Mark's Square.

Venice is encrusted with imagination. Its stones creak beneath an impressive pile of apparitions. There isn't another place in the world that could bear all that visionary tonnage on its shoulders. The recurring alarms concerning the survival of the city don't concern the architectural structures. With a bit of support from everybody, they might be able to survive. Instead, Venice will sink under the weight of all the visions, fantasies, stories, characters and daydreams it has inspired.

 · *eyes*

PUT ON VERY DARK SUNGLASSES: protect yourself. Venice can be lethal. In the historic centre the aesthetic radioactivity is extremely high. Every angle radiates beauty; apparently shabby: profoundly devious, inexorable. The sublime pours in bucketloads from the churches, but even the *calli* without monuments, the bridges to the *rii*, are picturesque at the very least. The façades of the *palazzi* are blows of the face, as kicks are blows of the feet. You are face-butted, slapped, abused by beauty. Andrea Palladio topples you over. Baldassare Longhena lays you flat. Mauro Codussi and Jacopo Sansovino finish you off. You feel terrible. It's the famous illness of Monsieur Henri Beyle, a disorder known to history as Stendhal Syndrome.

Don't make the situation worse, stop running after statues and paintings: among the countless works and collections that you constantly risk running into, I'll point out the ones that have been the city's two most deadly aesthetic experiences for me: one fairly obvious; another much more dangerous, because I didn't know anything about it and was slain unawares. When I want to hurt myself, I go and see the tumultuous cycle by Vittore Carpaccio at the Scuola di San Giorgio degli Schiavoni, which puts me in a brief coma every time. But while I was wandering around the Scuola Grande di San Rocco, certain that the innocuous Tintoretto couldn't make me sprout so much as an aesthetic boil, I had an apopleptic attack before the enchanting wooden reliefs of Francesco Pianta: extremely mysterious, kneaded with metaphors, pounded with symbols, a baroque binge that no one ever talks about.

If it only takes a few hours' stroll to take you to this state, think what the Venetians would have to say on the subject. The tourists are lucky: the moment they find themselves confronted by a splendid piece of architecture, they neutralise the aesthetic radioactivity by boxing it away in a camera. And what about the inhabitants? Too much splendour seriously damages your health. Constantly exposed to the wonders from morning till evening, the poor Venetian eyes absorb the aesthetic radioactivity, otherwise known as pulchroactivity. The *radium pulchritudinis* enfeebles them, strips them of all vital force, numbs them, depresses them. Not for nothing have the Venetians always been called Serenissimi: which is to say morbidly calm, stupefied, sleepwalkers. In a novel by Henry James, a London anarchist travels to Europe; in Venice he is overwhelmed by the beauty of the city, the Veronese ceilings change his life; he comes back to London for an assassination, but by now he has abandoned his career as a terrorist: he was supposed to kill a duke, and instead he suddenly commits suicide.

Luckily the twentieth century came up with some brilliant antidotes to the disease. The first remedy, mild and temporary but very widespread, is the restorers' scaffolding, wrapped with synthetic fabrics, or actually reinforced with solid wooden laths. That's why the restorations take so long: they're just an excuse to keep the deadly façades hidden for as long as possible. The scaffoldings are a kind of nuclear moratorium, like the ones they have on atomic missile testing: in Venice they serve to dam the devastating energy of the nuclear façades.

The other method, the one that involves building, is more radical, but sadly less practicable: there's no space left in the city to build as much as a dog's kennel. Venice is constipated with the past, and its past is sadly stupendous. So, as soon as the opportunity presents itself, the architects think about bringing a bit of relief to Venetian pupils. Take the vaporetto that runs along the Grand Canal: as if four kilometres of *palazzo* along the 'S' of water weren't enough, at the end the canal opens up into St Mark's Basin: you've barely left the Basilica della Salute and the Punta della Dogana behind you, and still lying in wait are the Island of San Giorgio, on the right, and on the left the Zecca, the Biblioteca Marciana, the Torre dell'Orologio, St Mark's Basilica, the Campanile, the Doge's Palace, the Bridge of Sighs, the Prisons! You're at bursting point, so much grace is about to deliver the *coup de grâce*, when at the very last minute the façade of the Hotel Danieli decides to come to your rescue, you recover by taking refuge in this comfortable bunker of horribleness. How could you survive San Moisè, were the Hotel Bauer Grünwald not next door? Thank you from the bottom of my heart, contemporary architects, thank you from the depths of my pupils for the headquarters of the Savings Bank in Campo Manin, for INPS and ASL and ENEL, for INAIL in Calle Nova di San Simón.

That's why the city is so devoted to Santa Lucia, St Lucy, the patron saint of sight. Every year, on the 13th of December, people go to the church of San Geremia, behind the altar, queue up along the crystal bier and pray beside the saint's mummy. Until the sixties, you could look Lucy straight in the sockets. The Venetians and the saint exchanged a salutary glance: exorbitant eyes, bulging with emotion, faced absent eyes, extracted when she was martyred. It was thought to be healing to open your eyelids wide in front of Lucia's empty cavities: the pupils of the Venetians wept, beauty-clouded crystalline lenses were washed clean, sinning retinas purified of the radioactive waste stored up in the course of a year in the city. Horror gave absolution to beauty: there was nothing macabre in any of this. Sadly the patriarch Albino Luciani, pastor of souls with nervous dispositions, some years before becoming Pope John Paul I and revealing to the whole of Christendom that God is the Mother, arranged for the face of the saint to be covered by a silver mask with pretty features.

Venice is based on a corpse. A thousand years ago, the theft of the remains of St Mark guaranteed the city's independence. That might explain the presence of so many mummies, to be venerated in their glass cases: St Lucy, but also St John the Almsgiver in the church of San Giovanni in Bragora; a pair of Egyptian corpses in the Archaeological Museum in St Mark's Square; the sarcophagus of Nehmekhet and some Armenian presbyters, with their nostrils dilated to extract the brain during the embalming process, on the island of San Lazzaro degli Armeni; and a prodigious priestess of crocodiles in the Natural History Museum in the

Fondaco dei Turchi. The priestess is laid out in the midst of a zoo of stuffed animals and a collection of weapons, everyday instruments and works of art from nineteenth-century Africa. She was brought to the city by the most neglected, the most unfortunate, the least celebrated of the legendary Venetian travellers. In the middle of the nineteenth century, in fact, it wasn't only the British and the French who went in search of the sources of the Nile: Giovanni Miani nearly got there, bartering glass beads from Murano (*'contarìe'*) halfway across Africa, enduring dysentery and floods and international boycotts and mockery at home, extracting his own teeth, riding on a bull after the death of his donkey, quelling the diversionary manoeuvres of suspicious natives, thwarting the nocturnal escapes of bearers. He fell ill a few days' walk from Lake Nyanza and did an about-turn: he planned to go back, but a few years later Speke and Grant beat him to it.

This is how Miani describes the case:

> Within the glass there can be seen a Mummy with a gilded face. This was found in the cave near Manfalut, above the Arabian mountain chain, where millions of embalmed crocodiles are found. Passing through this grotto I found human bodies buried among the great reptiles as seen here. Having undressed it here, we know that it is a Mummy of a woman, so we believe it was one of the

priestesses, mentioned by Herodotus, that fed the sacred amphibians, and when they died they were buried together.

Now close your eyes and imagine Venice razed to the ground: not so much as a brick, only the shades of the *calli* have been left standing, the pools of light of the *campi*. Pass through this fantastical urban chiaroscuro setting: streets of compact, viscous shadow; squares of exploded, pulverised light. Remember that this is the city that invented Venetian blinds, those curtains made of rotating horizontal sticks that slice the sunlight. The windows of the houses are exaggeratedly close to the corners, they struggle to lean further than they can manage towards the angular prow of the buildings to capture the greatest possible amount of light, to reflect it to the adjacent wall and back into the room.

Put on your reading glasses and read the streets. The names of the *calli*, bridges and *campi* are painted up on the walls. Black letters on white rectangles, above a layer of mortar: they are called *nissioéti* (or *nizioléti*: either way, it means 'little sheets'). Periodically, council workers come by with paint and brush: they aren't scrupulous philologists, sometimes they Italianise as they write. That's the only way of explaining how on earth the same *campo* comes to be named in two different ways only a few metres apart: Santa Margherita and Santa Margarita;

Santi Giovanni e Paolo, in one more archaic *nissioéto* they feature as Siamese saints: San Zanipolo, a kind of 'John Paul'.

Now sit down and learn this little toponomastic glossary:

There is only one *strada*, Strada Nóva, laid out (i.e. flattened) in the late nineteenth century to simplify the labyrinth of Cannaregio, copying in miniature the Haussmannian anti-barricade boulevards in Paris;

two *vie*, Via XXII Marzo in San Marco and Via Garibaldi in Castello: the *calli* around Via Garibaldi are spectacular parades of sheets, great buntings of undergarments, festoons of knickers stretching from one façade to the other, sometimes diagonally across the *campielli*, on washing lines tens of metres long;

liste are main streets and *crosère* are crossroads;

all the rest, or almost, are *calli* (and excuse me, they're always feminine: la *calle*, le *calli*); but there are also *rami* and *rughe*, not necessarily narrower (or more run-down!) than the *calli*;

and why are some *calli* not called *calli*, but *salizade*? *Salizada* means a paved street, *selciata* in Italian; originally the *calli* were beaten earth, the first paved *calli* were so identified to distinguish them from the ones that weren't yet paved: *salizada*, in short, is a fossil attribute that has survived the centuries;

a *rio terà* is a buried *rio* (*rio interrato*), that is, a canal that has become a *calle*;

the *fondamenta* (plural *fondamente*) is the walkable shore, that is, a *calle* with the houses on one side and a *rio* on the other; facing wider waters, the Grand Canal or St Mark's Basin, a *fondamenta* can end up being called a *riva*;

canali are the Grand Canal and the Giudecca Canal, wide and deep; almost all the others are *rii*; a few are broader stretches of water, the *bacini*, the *dàrsene*, the *piscine*;

the *ponti* are bridges, and there are about five hundred of them;

there's only one *piazza*, Piazza San Marco, St Mark's Square; all the others are *campi* or *campielli*; in memory of these *campi*'s former lives as meadows, in the summer interstitial plants grow between the cracks of the *maségni*; the only *campo* not yet cobbled, still covered with verdant green, is at San Pietro di Castello;

the *corti* are hidden *campielli*, inside groups of houses, they can be reached by only one entrance, a *calletta* or *sotopòrtego*;

the *sotopòrtego* ('*sottoportico*') is a passageway running between houses;

while we're about it, two more technical terms for

architectural features and places that you won't find written up on the *nissioéti*: *altana* is a wooden balcony built above the roof; it rests on slender, dizzying little columns of brick; *squèro* is the boatyard.

End of glossary.

Now that you know the dictionary of common street names you're ready to confront the encyclopaedia of proper names.

With a few exceptions, mostly to do with the Risorgimento or the postbellum, such as Via Garibaldi, Campo Manin and Campo Nazario Sauro, Venetian place-names reject the lay cult of personality. The streets are hardly ever dedicated to famous men and women, doges or admirals, travellers or musicians, but more often to foul deeds and popular customs, ordinary jobs and consumer products. Check the bibliography in the last chapter, and whatever you do, try and get hold of a guide to the hundreds of bizarre names of the *calli*. It's a different way of crossing the city: each *calle* condenses within its name an incredible microhistory. It's like reading *True Confessions* printed on the walls.

I can't sum them up as I'd like to, there are too many of them and they're too beautiful. I'll choose just one story, which will allow me to mention three *nissioéti*.

Five hundred years ago, spoon in hand, a workman is emptying his bowl of *sguaséto*, a kind of stew: among the tripe, lungs, spleen and oxtail wallowing about in the sauce, there's a mouthful that refuses to be chewed. It's a piece of finger, with the nail still attached. So that's what happened to all those children who disappeared in San Simeone! The workman reports the man who sold him the stew, the *luganaghèr* Biagio: the sausage-maker confesses, and is dragged along the ground tied to the tail of a horse, flaying himself on the long journey from jail to the shop; here his hands are cut off; on the return journey, so as not to waste time, he is tortured with pincers; the hooded executioner, rumoured to live incognito in Calle della Testa, (*Calle* of the Head), beheads him between the two columns of St Mark's; the body is cut into pieces, and the limbs are displayed to the citizenry, for public edification, probably hung from the gallows of the Ponte dei Squartài (Bridge of the Quartered Men) over the Rio dei Tolentini, as is customary in such cases. The sausage-maker Biagio Cargnio, serial killer and cooker of children, is recalled by the *nissioéto* in the Riva di Biasio, at the beginning of the Grand Canal.

Generally speaking, there is a proliferation of *nissioéti* of *calli* dedicated to the old trade guilds. Those of the *campi*, on the other hand, tend to name saints. In Venice, work is narrow, religion wide.

The trades of the *calli* are fossils of a pre-Fordian

economy: Calle dei Botèri (coopers); Calle dei Saonèri (soap-makers); Calle dei Lavadori (washermen); Calle del Calderèr (a coppersmith); Calle dei Fusèri (spindle-makers); Calle dei Spezieri (spicers).

The saints of the *campi* are figures from the second and third strata of the celestial aristocracy: Sant'Aponàl, San Boldo, San Basegio, San Cassàn, Ss. Gervasio e Protasio, San Marcuola, San Provolo, San Stae, San Stin, San Trovaso. A little heavenly mafia has appropriated the airiest spaces, a theological *coup d'état* has dethroned the prince of Paradise, sending him into exile from the holy reaches, sticking him in the dampest and most unhealthy passageways, amidst the lowly shopkeepers and craftsmen: Christ and the Cross suffocate in a dozen secondary *callette*.

Now that you've got used to keeping your face turned upwards, watch out for meteorites: pigeon droppings, of course, and not only that. A real cloudburst can bring down square metres of wet plaster. Examples of large-scale collapses in Venice in recent years: a trader on his way to work in the Merceria is thrown to the ground, struck by a moulding that suddenly broke away from the first floor of a building above his head. A whole wall fell into the water in Rio della Toletta, parting the brick curtain to reveal a couple of baffled tenants, sprawled on the sofa in front of the TV in their slippers and underwear: lucky that there wasn't a boat going past at that moment! A piece of balcony fell to the ground in the middle of Campo San Luca. A big plate from the metal cover of San Simón Piccolo came loose, entangled itself in the cornice of the cupola, and remained hanging like a guillotine of Damocles, balanced twenty metres above the necks of the pedestrians. A block of white Istrian stone, thirty kilos in weight, fell from the arch of one of the windows of the Doge's Palace: as it hit the ground, a splinter injured a German tourist.

There are endless popular anecdotes about tiles, bits of plaster, terracotta vases of impressive weight (*pitèri*) suddenly crashing on to the paving stones, geraniums and cyclamens shattering on the ground, or on the skulls of passers-by: scattering pottery, black soil, brain-matter, splinters, petals, false teeth, plant-feed, eyeballs. As in all the best traditions, La Serenissima has encouraged and institutionalised this characteristic city sport: at the Merceria an old bas-relief shows the treacherous old woman who, almost seven centuries ago, threw from her window sill a *pitèr*, a mortar or an earthenware pot on the head of the standard-bearer of Baiamonte Tiepolo, causing his militia to lose their bearings and defeating his conspiracy against Doge Gradenigo. One autumn afternoon I saw a man appear at a window in the Campo dei Frari: the shutter was fixed on a rusty hinge and fell on to the *fondamenta* a few centimetres from the head of a passer-by. Who said Venice was sinking? Venice is falling to bits.

Live animals fall like hailstones, too, domestic pussycats locked away at home by jealous old maids. During the season of love, the cats wail disconsolately from the balustrades of the balconies, sending passionate messages to the luckier strays. The street cats climb on top of each other in acrobatic formations: one on top of the other on top of the other. Tormented by these irresistible spectacles, the housebound felines can no longer contain themselves, their desire overflows beyond the balustrade: they hurl themselves from the second floor, their mistresses hunt for them irritably throughout the flat, and two weeks later back comes puss, covered with scratches and blissfully happy.

But the moment has come to immortalise the all-time world champion of the down-jump, the mythical Heideggerian cat of the Giudecca.

The tom in question, one Pucci, three-quarters of a century ago, loved to go to sleep on the window sill of a third-storey flat: basking – as they say – beatifically in the sun. To avoid being disturbed by anyone, Pucci would go out on to the balcony, climb on to the balustrade, jump from there on to the next window sill along and stretch out just outside the closed shutters. Whenever my great-grandmother opened the shutters, Pucci suddenly found himself disconcertedly in the void, miaowed with terror and, in a flash, adopted the pose of the flying squirrel, that acrobatic beast with planar membranes: cats are skilled fallers. The little boys playing in the *calle* always kept an eye on that third-floor window: every time they saw Pucci back on his window sill, they would wait half an hour, let the cat settle in his position, and then call my great-grandmother to the window, at which she would appear, throwing open the shutters.

People often wonder whether animals dream, whether they too are pursued by nightmares not dissimilar to our own, like the ones that end with a fall into the void, dreams that plunge deeper and deeper into themselves before plunging out into a comfortable awakening on our pillow. Let us now consider the experience of this Heideggerian cat which, emerging from a placid snooze, *opened his eyes on to the fall*. During those same years the philosopher Martin Heidegger explained that coming into the world is like being thrown, it is a fall of being, diving into time. Life is a cat asleep on the window sill suddenly waking as it falls from the third floor.

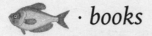 · *books*

F OR EVERY CHAPTER in this brief physical and emotional stroll, I shall suggest a few books that give a better explanation of some things than I have been able to, and also some which have nothing to do with Venice, but which I have happened to drag in for some reason or another.

But before anything else, you should know that the guide to Venice *par excellence*, still unsurpassed in quantity of information and details, is the classic *Venice and its Lagoon* by Giulio Lorenzetti (Edizioni Lint).

You'll find an overall image of contemporary Venice with plenty of advice on making the most of your free time in *Venezia, istruzioni per l'uso* by Aline Cendon and Giampaolo Simonetti (Marsilio).

To find out about the youth, old age and miracles of La Serenissima, entrust yourself immediately to *Venice: a Maritime Republic* by Frederic C. Lane (Johns Hopkins

University Press).

If you don't want to take quite so much trouble, an excellent synthesis is *La Breve Storia di Venezia* by Gherardo Ortalli and Giovanni Scarabello (Pacini Editore).

The birth of the city, with the documentation of the most recent archaeological studies, may be found in the monumental *Venezia Origini* by Wladimir Dorigo (Electa).

The novel by Bohumil Hrabal with the nail-hammering child is *I Served the King of England* (Picador).

I stole the information about the submarine plantations of tree trunks from the splendid books of Paolo Barbaro, along with many other hints and data: *Venezia, l'anno del mare felice* (il Mulino) and *Venezia. La città ritrovata* (Marsilio).

A systematic treatment of Venetian building techniques may be found in *Venezia nei secoli* by Eugenio Miozzi (Libeccio).

feet

In *Guida sentimentale di Venezia* (Passigli), Diego Valeri also advised wandering at random: 'Strolling about *calli* and *campi*, without a pre-established itinerary, is perhaps the greatest pleasure you can have in Venice.'

The French gentleman who remembered for the rest of his life the slight unevenness in the Venetian paving stones beneath his feet is of course Marcel Proust, *In Search of Lost Time* (Penguin).

legs

The torture of hope is related in one of the *Cruel Tales* of Villiers de l'Isle-Adam.

Josef Brodsky, in *Watermark* (Penguin), is struck by the balancing act performed by the legs when trying to remain upright on Venetian vessels.

All the secrets of the lagoon ecosystem are illustrated in *La laguna di Venezia*, ed. Giovanni Caniato, Eugenio Turri, Michele Zanetti (Cierre), and in *La laguna*, ed. S. Giordani (Corbo e Fiore); there's also the *Guida alla natura nella laguna di Venezia* by Giampaolo Rallo (Muzzio).

Books about boats: Gilberto Penzo, *Barche veneziane* (Libreria Editrice Il Leggio); Carlo Donatelli, *La gondola* (Arsenale).

The clearest description of the causes of the *acqua alta* and the various projects to safeguard the city may be found in *Dove volano I leoni* by Gianfranco Bettin (Garzanti).

heart

The polemic between Tadeusz Zulawskij and Isaak Abrahamowitz is recorded in issue 33 of the journal *Pàthema*, June 1997.

The interview with Oskar Krickstein appears in issue 48 of the American monthly *SuperMuscle*, April 1997.

The untitled poem by Costanza Fenegoni Varotti is taken from the collection *Laguna ardente* (Edizioni del Crepuscolo; I should like to thank the author for her kind permission).

The line by Andrea Zanzotto is from the poem 'Ormai', from the collection *Dietro il paesaggio* (Mondadori).

hands

Monographs devoted entirely to types of Venetian rowlock: Gilberto Penzo, *Forcole, remi e voga alla veneta* (Libreria Editrice Il Leggio); *Forcole*, ed. Saverio Pàstor (Il Leggio e Mare di Carta Libreria Nautica).

face

One of the texts richest in information and illustrations on ways of camouflaging oneself in Venice is the one by Danilo Reato, *Le maschere veneziane* (Arsenale); for an economical synthesis: Lina Urban, *Le maschere di Carnevale a Venezia* (Edizioni Turismo Veneto).

The novel in which Henry James describes Venice as the interior of an apartment is *The Aspern Papers* (Penguin).

ears

The hidden gardens of Venice were unearthed by Gianni Berengo Gardin, Cristiana Moldi Ravenna and Teodora Sammartini *(I Giardini nascosti a Venezia,* Arsenale).

The blind writer who 'sees' the city thanks to bad weather is John M. Hull, *Touching the Rock* (Vintage).

mouth

The phoneticist Luciano Canepari has come up with an elegant method of transcribing Venetian sounds, applying it amongst other things to the lyrics of lagoon-based reggae, funk and salsa bands such as Pitura Freska, Zoo Zabumba and Batisto Coco. To avoid getting out of my depth, however, I have chosen not to follow him in this book.

For the flavours of the lagoon, consult and keep in your kitchen the classic *A tola co i nostri veci* by Mariù Salvatori de Zuliani (Franco Angeli Editore). Just one slight problem: it's written in Venetian!

On the old *bàcari*: Elio Zorzi, *Osterie veneziane* (Filippi Editore).

A series of very intelligent tips concerning bars and other delectable ways of spending time in the city can be found in *Venezia, osterie e dintorni* by Michela Scibilia (Libreria Sansovino).

nose

Hundreds of Venetian proverbs have been collected by Giovanni Antonio Cibotto (*Proverbi del Veneto*, Giunti).

A study of the games of Venetian street urchins can be found in *I giochi di quando eravamo piccolo. A Venezia, a Trieste, in Friuli*, by Andrea Penso (Corbo e Fiore).

The celebrated passage in the *Divine Comedy* in which Dante compares the pitch of the shipyards with the pitch that boils the souls of the barrators appears in *Inferno*, XXI, 7–21.

Madonna Lisetta Querini is the silly girl convinced that she's going to bed with 'the Angel Gabriel' in the Venetian story in the *Decameron*, IV, 2.

As everybody knows, Shakespeare was a copycat. His *Othello*, which has, apart from anything else, only one scene set in Venice, is plagiarised from the sixteenth-century story of the Moor of Venice told in the

Hecatommithi (III, 7) by the Ferrarese writer Giambattista Giraldi Cinzio.

Countess Livia, the protagonist of *Senso* by Camillo Boito, owes her surname Serpieri to the eponymous film by Luchino Visconti.

Miss Bordereau wastes away in Venice in *The Aspern Papers* by Henry James, quoted above.

Aschenbach is the famous tourist in *Death in Venice* by Thomas Mann (and, once again, Luchino Visconti).

Andreas or the United is Hugo von Hofmannsthal's Venetian novella.

These are ultra-classical authors, you'll find almost all of them in various editions.

Finally, Colin comes to a nasty end before the eyes of Mary in *The Comfort of Strangers* by Ian McEwan (Vintage): in that novel the city is described with great accuracy but never named.

eyes

In the mid-nineteenth century, John Ruskin built a famous monument of words on the architecture of Venice: *The Stones of Venice* builds up the Gothic and demolishes the Renaissance.

The other novel by Henry James, with the repentant terrorist, is *Princess Casamassima*.

Aldo Andreolo and Elisabetta Brosetti have transcribed all the memorial plaques in the city in *Venezia ricorda. I volti, le vite e le opera dei veneziani e dei 'foresti' che la città ha voluto ricordare nel marmo* (Le Altane).

All the secrets of the *nissioéti* are revealed in the monumental *Curiosità veneziane* by Giuseppe Tassini (Filippi Editore), which is rather costly but indispensable: it's now also available in a handy paperback edition; Paolo Piffarerio and Piero Zanotto have put together a nice comic-strip edition in two volumes, *I nizioleti raccontano* (Edizioni Hunter) and *I nizioleti raccontano 2* (Il Cardo).

The great nineteenth-century pulp writer Giuseppe Tassini, an erudite, hedonistic and affable womaniser, also left us *Alcune delle più clamorose condanne capitali* and *Il libertinaggio a Venezia* (Filippi Editore).

The quotation about the mummy is taken from Giovanni Miani, *Le spedizioni alle origini del Nilo*, published in Venice by Gaetano Longo in 1865: you'll only find it in Venetian libraries (I consulted it in Venice's big public library, the Querini Stampalia).

A thrilling reconstruction of Miani's travels through his diaries was recently written by Graziella Civiletti, *Un veneziano in Africa* (ERI Edizioni Rai).

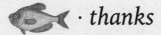 · *thanks*

THANKS to Ernani, Maria and Daniele Scarpa; to Paolo Verri, who had the idea for this book, and to Edia Manente who persuaded me to write it; to Alberto Rollo, who suggested its title (and not just that).

Thanks also to Stefano Bassanese, Marco Belpoliti, Daria Bignardi, Casimiro Di Crescenzo, Costanza Fenegoni Varotti, Roberto Ferrucci, Antonella Fiori, Aurora Fonda, Alessandra Galletta, Cristiana Giacometti, Giuliana Giampietro, Daniela Lotta, Diogo Mainardi, Vittorio Marchiori, Raul Montanari, Antonio Moresco, Mauro Mussolin, Enrico Ratti, Piero Vereni.

 · *coda*

WHAT FOLLOWS IS A micro-anthology of Venetian texts. They're only a few pages long, but they refer to the three statistically most widespread ways of being in Venice: as a foreign tourist (Maupassant); as a foreign resident (Mainardi); as an emigrated native (me).

1. The article *Venice* by Guy de Maupassant was published in *Gil Blas* on 5th May 1885. I chose it because it gave me an excuse to translate a few pages by one of my favourite writers, and because in a few lines it includes all the fundamental impressions you feel in Venice.

Above all, the sense of linguistic incrustation, the accumulation of opinions and descriptions that came before us. Then comes the discovery of the dirty water, and the actual smallness of the city in relation to the vastness of its fame. I am reminded of a story by J G Ballard: in 2001 the time machine has been invented, the television channels pick up the most important historical events and broadcast them internationally, but after an initial euphoria the public is disappointed by the unspectacular nature of the crucial events of human history. In this sense Maupassant is travelling in a mythical space machine. He is in a paradoxical situation, like everyone who comes to Venice: the myth attracts him and challenges him to peel away the mythical film that envelops the very myth itself, to end up producing a modernised form of the myth and thus ensure its perpetuation. It is the typical trap of myth-makers, or rather, that's how myths are mythographically maintained.

It's interesting to note how Maupassant's writing suffocates in superlatives and the rather sickly adjectival eulogy when he has to pay the usual descriptive toll to monumental beauty. Even more interesting that Maupassant should choose the 'elegant and coquettish' Giambattista Tiepolo, the lightest of the Venetian painters. Tiepolo is the painter who, as Maupassant writes, might be admired less than the others, but is liked all the more. The French writer finds in his painting a relief from the aesthetic burden of Venice, still seeking at the same time to find in art an antidote to art. Cultural duty imposes a deference to beauty: Maupassant doesn't feel like leaving the museum, he just goes and gets a breath of fresh air in its coolest corner.

2. The story 'The Killing Stones' was written for RadioRai in the form of a mini radio drama, and was broadcast on 30th June 1997 in the series *Sintonie*. In 1999 it was published in *Zona. Scritture dal territorio* (Editrice Zona, Genoa). I've considerably revised it here.

3. *Instructions for self-defence against beauty* is a remix of several paragraphs in the chapter *Eyes*. It was published in a more succinct form in *L'Unità*, 5th August 1996. I owe the idea of the remix in literature to the brilliant multiform idea of Tommaso Labranca. The greatest musical remix artists around at the moment are the Austrians Kruder & Dorfmeister and, in England, Fatboy Slim.

4. *The Bridge of Gum* is a remix of the paragraph on the Ponte del Vinante in the chapter *Hands*. It was written in 1993. It hasn't been published before.

5. *Going Back to Sleep in Venice* by the Brazilian writer Diogo Mainardi was published in 1995 in the pamphlet in five languages distributed to young tourists staying in Venice, edited by Roberto Ferruccia and myself, published by the Assessorato alla gioventù del commune di Venezia as part of the project *Rolling (writing) Venice*.

V

 · *venice*

Guy de Maupassant

V ENICE! IS THERE A CITY more admired, more celebrated, more sung by the poets, more desired by lovers, more visited and more illustrious?

Venice! Is there a name in all the languages of humanity that makes us dream more than that one? It is pretty, besides, sonorous and sweet; all at once it calls to mind a dazzling procession of magnificent memories, a whole horizon of enchanting reveries.

Venice! That single word seems to send an exaltation exploding in the soul, it excites everything poetic within us, it provokes all our faculties of admiration. And when we arrive in this unique city, we inevitably study it with forewarned and ravished eyes, we look upon it with our dreams.

For it is almost impossible for a man who travels the world not to mingle his imagination with the vision of reality. Travellers are accused of lying and deceiving their readers. No, they don't lie, but they see with their thoughts rather than their eyes. It takes only a novel that has charmed us, twenty lines that have moved us, a story that has captivated us to prepare us for the special lyricism of these voyagers and, when we are thus excited from a distance by the desire for a country, it seduces us irresistibly. No corner of the globe has, more than Venice, given rise to this conspiracy of enthusiasm. When we first enter that vaunted lagoon, it is almost impossible to react against our anticipated feeling of disillusion. Anyone who has read, who has dreamed, who knows the history of the city he is entering, who is penetrated by all the opinions of those who came before him, brings with him his impressions almost all ready-made: he knows what he must love, what he must despise, what he must admire.

The train first crosses a plain riddled with curious puddles. It looks like a kind of map, with oceans and continents; then gradually the ground disappears; the convoy runs on to an embankment before launching out on an endless bridge thrown into the sea, which leads towards the city seen in the distance, its bell towers and monuments rising above the still and boundless sheet of water. A few islands bearing farms appear from time to time on either side.

We pull into the station. Gondolas wait along the quay. Long, thin and black, the tips at either end standing upright, bearing at the front a strange and pretty prow, in gleaming steel, the fine gondola deserves its glory. A man, standing behind his passengers, controls it with a single oar borne and supported by a kind of twisted wooden arm fixed to the right-hand side of the vessel. It looks at once coquettish and severe, loving and warlike, and it deliciously rocks the traveller stretched out on a kind of chaise longue. The gentleness of this seat, the exquisite sway of those boats, their lively, calm appearance, give us a sensation both unexpected and adorable. One does nothing and one moves, one rests and one sees, one is caressed by this movement, caressed in the spirit and in the flesh, filled with a sudden and continuous physical delight, and by a profound well-being of the soul. When it rains, a little room of sculpted wood, adorned with brass and covered with a black drape, is erected in the middle of these boats. Then the gondolas slide impenetrably, dark and closed, floating coffins dressed in crepe. They seem to carry mysteries of death or of love, and sometimes the pretty face of a woman appears behind their narrow window.

We go down the Grand Canal. We are surprised at first by the appearance of this city whose streets are rivers... rivers, or rather sewers open to the sky.

That is really the impression that Venice gives once the initial astonishment is past. It is as though facetious engineers had blown up the vault of masonry and paving stones that covers those dirty streams in all the other cities of the world, to force the inhabitants to sail on their sewers.

And yet some of those canals, the narrowest, can be deliciously bizarre. The old houses eaten away by poverty reflect their faded, blackened walls in them, dip into them their dirty, pitted feet, like poor, ragged people washing in streams. The stone bridges straddle this water, and as they cast their image into it they frame it in a double vault, one of which is false, the other real. One has dreamed a vast city with huge palaces, so great is the renown of this ancient queen of the seas. One is astonished to see it so tiny, tiny, tiny! Venice is but a knick-knack, a charming old artistic knick-knack, poor and ruined, but proud, beautifully proud, of its ancient glory.

Everything seems to be in ruins, everything seems on the point of collapsing into this water that bears an exhausted city. The palaces bear façades that are ravaged by time, stained by damp, eaten away by the leprosy that destroys the stones and marbles. Some tilt vaguely to the side, ready to fall, tired of staying so long upright on their piles. All of a sudden the horizon expands, the lagoon widens; there, on the right, appear islands covered with houses and, on the left, an admirable *palazzo* in the Moorish style, a marvel of oriental grace and imposing elegance, the Doge's Palace.

I shall not tell the Venice of which all the world has spoken. St Mark's Square looks like the Place du Palais-Royal, the church's façade looks like the papier-mâché frontage of a café-concert, but the interior is the most absolutely beautiful thing imaginable. The penetrating harmony of lines and tones, the reflections of the old golden mosaics with their soft brilliance, amidst severe marble, the wonderful proportions of arches and backgrounds, some *je-ne-sais-quoi* divinely judged within the whole, in the calm flood of daylight that assumes a religious quality around these pillars, in the sensation cast into the mind by the eyes, make St Mark's the most completely admirable thing in the world.

But as one contemplates this incomparable masterpiece of Byzantine art, one begins to dream, comparing it with another religious monument, it too unequalled but so very different, a masterpiece of Gothic art, built in the middle of the grey waves of the Northern seas, that monstrous granite jewel that stands alone in the vast bay of Mont-St-Michel.

What makes Venice absolutely without equal is

painting. Venice was the fatherland, the mother of some masters of the first rank who may be encountered only in her museums, her churches and her palaces. Only in Venice do Titian and Veronese reveal themselves in all their brilliant splendour. They at least have glory in all its power and breadth. There are others with whom we in France are none too familiar and who almost attain the worth of these artists, such as Carpaccio and especially Tiepolo, the foremost among all ceiling-painters, past, present and future. No one better than he knew how to spread on a wall the grace of human lines, the seductiveness of nuances that sensually intoxicate the eye, and the charm of things dreamt in that kind of strange drunkenness that art communicates to the mind. As elegant and coquettish as Watteau or Boucher, Tiepolo has above all an admirable and invincible ability to enchant. One may admire others more than him, with reasoned admiration, but one is more affected by him than by anyone. The brilliance of his compositions, the powerful, pretty unpredictability of his design, the variety of his ornamentation, the constant and unique freshness of his shades create within us a singular need to live for ever beneath one of the inestimable ceilings decorated by his hand.

The Palazzo Labia, a ruin, shows perhaps the most admirable thing left by this great artist. He painted a whole room, a vast room. He did everything, the ceiling, the walls, the decoration and the architecture, with his brush. The theme, the history of Cleopatra, an eighteenth-century Venetian Cleopatra, is continued on the four walls of the apartment, passes through all the doors, beneath the marble, behind the imitation columns. The characters lie on the cornices, rest their arms or their feet on the ornamentations, peopling this place with their charming, brightly coloured crowd. The *palazzo* containing this masterpiece is said to be for sale! Imagine how one might live there!

· *the killing stones*

DR HOFFMANN: The first suicide was on Friday, the fifteenth of April, between four and six in the morning.

INSPECTOR: At least that was what the post-mortem established.

DR HOFFMANN: Pathologists tend not to rely on guess-work. Or do we wish to begin by maligning your colleagues, Inspector?

INSPECTOR: God forbid. Especially since you yourself are one of my colleagues... And I have a sense that you will remain so for some time, given the special nature of the case.

DR HOFFMANN: Of all these cases, I would say.

INSPECTOR: Hmm... Let's stick with this one for the time being.

DR HOFFMANN: The suicide hanged himself from one of the statues on the façade of the church of the Barefoot Friars.

INSPECTOR: It had just been restored.

DR HOFFMANN: The scaffolding had been taken down two days before. It took years to clean the blackened stone. An extremely lengthy task that involved the consolidation of the structures, but at last the temple has been restored to its baroque magnificence.

INSPECTOR: A spectacle to take your breath away.

DR HOFFMANN: Bear in mind that this monument is the first to loom above the tourists as they leave the railway station: they are obliged to pass before it as soon as they set foot in the city.

INSPECTOR: At any rate, the corpse was hanging from a rope attached to the neck of a saint.

DR HOFFMANN: As though he wished to impersonate a kind of human failure suspended from a matchless model. The corpse of a mortal suspended from the incorruptible statue of a saint!

INSPECTOR: And according to your theory...

DR HOFFMANN: According to my theory, the choice of hanging and the place of the suicide, on the very threshold of the city as far as foreigners are concerned, sends out a very clear message.

INSPECTOR: 'A toll of horror to be paid to beauty by those who enter Venice', you have written.

DR HOFFMANN: Exactly so. You are much more scrupulous than my pupils. You reach my conclusions precisely.

INSPECTOR: And to come to the second case...

DR HOFFMANN: As I see it, the second case has aspects that are symbolically even more elaborate. Suicide, we know, is always a form of communication.

INSPECTOR: Even when one kills oneself without leaving as much as a note?

DR HOFFMANN: But of course. Self-destruction is an extreme discourse that the suicide was unable to express in any other way. It would appear that killing oneself is simpler than expressing the terrible truth about one's own condition.

INSPECTOR: This time the suicide chained his wrists and ankles to a mooring post sunk in the Grand Canal.

DR HOFFMANN: On the night of the ninth of May, that's right. It would appear that he waited for the tide to rise until it submerged him completely. He allowed himself to drown. A horrible death!

INSPECTOR: And quite an imaginative one.

DR HOFFMANN: I don't think we should discharge our cynicism on some poor corpse.

INSPECTOR: That would be *my* cynicism. Forgive me, I thought that the imperturbable scientific spirit liked to appreciate the more ruthless sides of reality.

DR HOFFMANN: You have a rather old-fashioned idea of us scientists. But we aren't here to talk about me. Turning to our second unfortunate, note that the mooring post in question was...

INSPECTOR: ...behind a jetty of the Ca' d'Oro. Another monument recently restored.

DR HOFFMANN: At this point I recalled a former patient of mine, another Venetian who committed suicide in similar circumstances some years ago.

INSPECTOR: Did you know him well?

DR HOFFMANN: Barely at all. He had been entrusted to my care about three days before his death.

INSPECTOR: Too late even for a miracle-worker!

DR HOFFMANN: Quite. I certainly have no illusions of having given him a good reason to live. To be honest, I didn't even have time to understand the true reasons behind his self-destructive impulses.

INSPECTOR: However, you were able to examine his papers after the fact.

DR HOFFMANN: His family let me have his diary. Reading it, I discovered that the man was obsessed by the beauty of Venice. This city gave him a sense of unbearable suffocation.

INSPECTOR: A form of Stendhal Syndrome.

DR HOFFMANN: Not really... That's the psychology of the television news report. And take care not to confuse occasional bouts of indigestion with permanent intoxication. Stendhal Syndrome can afflict those unprepared tourists who arrive in Venice, leaving behind them the ugliness of their suburbs, where dormitories are built that resemble graveyards for the living dead. Once one has arrived in Venice, it is almost obvious that an individual accustomed to that kind of landscape feels a sudden lack. Clearly, he is incapable of bearing in such massive doses the vast quantity of beauty that the city pours on top of him all at once. But to go from there to taking one's own life... Well, there's nothing to stop him packing his bags and going back home to take a good deep breath of foul air amongst his beloved exhaust pipes.

INSPECTOR: While an inhabitant of Venice...

DR HOFFMANN: An inhabitant of Venice must bear on his shoulders, throughout the whole of his life, the burden of this enormous aesthetic tonnage. This former patient of mine felt like a rat in a trap, strangled by the enchantment of *calli* a metre wide... Those little streets leave no escape route for the eye, it is crushed between a picturesque angle and an architectural epiphany, oppressed between the grace of a bridge and the shady sweetness of a passageway.

INSPECTOR: It's no coincidence that he was found in...

DR HOFFMANN: In Calle del Paradiso, the most sugges-
tive alleyway in the whole of Venice.

INSPECTOR: The bas-reliefs on the triangular
architrave, the panoramic beams that jut from the
buttresses... It's very beautiful, yes, perhaps the most
beautiful of all.

DR HOFFMANN: But for him, clearly, it was the most lethal.

INSPECTOR: In this case, too, restoration work had been
carried out. The *calle* had recently been reopened to
pedestrians.

DR HOFFMANN: In fact, in all three cases we are dealing
with monuments that had been covered up for some
time. Which had made them, so to speak, more
endurable, more human. When the scaffolding was
removed, on the other hand, for those individuals
already in a state of profound exasperation it was as
though an aesthetic tide carried along by its native
energy were surging through everything, unhindered...
In each case, beauty delivered the *coup de grâce*.

INSPECTOR: But the man found in Calle del Paradiso
had poisoned himself.

DR HOFFMANN: Yes, but the true poison was adminis-
tered by the city itself.

INSPECTOR: So you're saying that Venice is a kind of serial killer.

DR HOFFMANN: You do me the honour of quoting the formula – catchy, I acknowledge – that found a certain resonance in the media. In fact, this happy expression appeared in passing in a much more well-constructed scientific context.

INSPECTOR: Which received a gratifying reaction at the world psychiatry conference in Pittsburgh last spring.

DR HOFFMANN: That report did enjoy some success amongst my transatlantic colleagues, yes.

INSPECTOR: And it consecrated you as one of the most original psychotherapists of the present day. After a career which has been, if you will forgive me, less than dazzling.

DR HOFFMANN: On the contrary. Unlike the police, we don't need connections to win competitions and obtain promotions.

INSPECTOR: Really?

DR HOFFMANN: The course of my career as a student and a therapist has always been marked by the most scrupulous professionalism, and besides, I don't see what parameters you might have at your disposal to assess the quality of the...

INSPECTOR: Yes, yes, but I'm not talking about your career as a doctor of the mind. Before specialising in psychiatry, as a young man you tried a quite different career. My suspicions were aroused by all those references to building techniques, those architectural metaphors that appear in your report. Dr Hoffmann, you are a failed architect.

DR HOFFMANN: How do you know that!

INSPECTOR: I discovered it over time, between one request for a reference and another. I found some of your old articles. The ones in which you sought to demonstrate the absurdity of any kind of restoration, to the point of proposing the systematic demolition of historic buildings, just to resolve the problem at its root.

DR HOFFMANN: I don't see what that has to do with it.

INSPECTOR: Who knows? I remember your essay about the Campanile of St Mark's, which collapsed at the beginning of the twentieth century and was rebuilt by the Venetians applying the motto, *as it was, where it was*. 'To think of rebuilding something only remotely related to the original is madness. It should be razed to the ground.' Am I misquoting, doctor?

DR HOFFMANN: You are quoting from something written many years ago.

INSPECTOR: And what of your euphoric declarations

about the fire at La Fenice? 'I am not afraid to be alone in rejoicing amidst the many hypocrites who are rending their garments. At last a major building to be rebuilt *ex novo*. I hope that this city's funereal obsession will not lead to the insane proposition of rebuilding the theatre just as it was. Let us cease being slaves of the dead, tied to the putrefied aesthetics of our forefathers. They had no scruples! Did they respect the Gothic, or the Neo-Classicists? Would we have had the Baroque if the sixteenth century had doggedly repeated the Renaissance? With the fire at La Fenice, a gap has opened for the Futurist utopia!'

DR HOFFMANN: Journalistic exaggerations. Never trust their verbatim quotes. In any case, I'm not an architect any more.

INSPECTOR: You were never able to become one, because of Venice. You hate this place; you have never forgiven the city its *palazzi*, its *rii*, *calli* and *fondamente*, its churches and *sottoportici*. You were brought here from Berlin at the age of seven, you grew up in a place flooded with monuments, churches and historic buildings. A city where there is no room to build anything else, just to restore, repair, renew, respecting the old, venerating the ancient, adoring the decrepit. A city where you have to renounce the idea of expressing anything truly unfamiliar, rather than leaving a trace as in any other city in the world, rather than marking your passage on earth with your own little milestone.

DR HOFFMANN: You see? What you're describing would be an unbearable situation for an architect!

INSPECTOR: A condition that can lead to madness. Or inflicting it on others. By a quirk of fate, throughout these years the city of your birth has become a permanent building-site. When you realised that your Berlin had become a paradise for architects... Whole districts disembowelled and remodelled!

DR HOFFMANN: Potsdamer Platz redesigned from top to bottom, playfully distorted...

INSPECTOR: You couldn't bear it. You killed three men who had nothing to fear from the beauty of the stones of Venice. You made them victims of your self-destructive aesthetic obsession. You even managed to theorise a new psychical pathology, becoming famous at the expense of your victims. You became the speculators' idol, you supplied arguments and justifications for the worst kind of building ventures. And above all, you took your revenge on Venice, accusing the city of being the most ruthless serial killer of its own inhabitants. You may call your lawyer, Dr Hoffmann.

· *instructions for self-defence against beauty*

THE STEEL TUBES of the scaffolding around buildings in the process of restoration are wrapped in silver-grey or dark green synthetic fabrics. These materials have replaced the old soft rush mats and clear plastic tarpaulins. For prolonged restorations, temporary authentic pseudo-façades are built with wooden laths. We call them temporary even if they can remain in place for several years. The pseudo-façades are rectangular or box-shaped structures with lots of glass windows. They look a bit like the buildings of Aldo Rossi: like the floating wooden World Theatre that was anchored to the Punta della Dogana during the 1979 Biennale.

In Venice, when they cover the façades of churches and *palazzi*, the pseudo-façades, whether in synthetic materials or in wood, have the great merit of protecting the eyes of the residents. If a façade is, as etymology suggests, a face-butt, a blow delivered by the face, this is not to disregard the fact that the inhabitants of Venice are ceaselessly exposed to these bruising visions. We cannot hope to survive unharmed on an aesthetic diet of daily poisoning through beauty. It would be improper to put the question in terms of Stendhal Syndrome: ingesting daily visual doses of *calli, fondamente, campielli, canali* and *rii* cannot be compared to the casual indigestions of beauty to which occasional tourists are subjected. The places from which the *foresti* (outsiders) come are for the most part urban fabrics where smog and basilicas, barracks and the baroque, traffic lights and *campanili* are cleverly woven into a disharmonic order. The Venetians, on the other hand, grow up amidst an excess of beauty without having at their disposal the instruments of defence that tourists can command. No one has ever seen a Venetian, fearing an attack of aesthetic apoplexy at the sight of the Ca' d'Oro or the Bridge of Sighs, promptly whip out a camera. And yet these are places that one may have to pass by several times a day. Let us bear in mind that in Venice it is not only the most famous monuments that are targeted by the tourists' lenses. The whole city knows the click of cameras and the hum of video cameras: a sign that almost every *rio, calle* or *riva* that can be walked upon beside a canal (*fondamenta*), every *campiello* and bridge emanates, radiates and overflows with beauty.

How many pulchroactive places are there in Rome or Florence? Twenty-five, seventy-seven, a hundred and eleven? In Venice such a count isn't even imaginable: like the Geiger counters in Chernobyl in 1986, Baumgarten-counters in Venice crackle far beyond the tolerance threshold, revealing an intense level of pulchroactivity throughout the whole of the city: what is interesting is not so much the fact that surveys reach frequent peaks of *sublime*, as that median values never fall below *picturesque*. Testimony is provided by the so-called 'lesser Venice' portrayed by the nineteenth-century realistic painters: not the inflated views of St Mark's Square, of Canalettian descent, but the humble glimpses of anonymous canals painted by such artists as Rubens Santoro, Alessandro Milesi, Giacomo Favretto, Pietro Fragiacomo, Guglielmo Ciardi.

There is no escape from such radiation. Tourists have a method of actively neutralising these places: they capture them in their cameras. As soon as the aesthetic sensor embodied in the tourist (normally set to *kitsch* mode) lights up, they immediately shield themselves against the *radium pulchritudinis* (or pulchroactivity) of the urban landscape, thus avoiding the danger of lethal contamination.

And what about the poor Venetians? It is well known

that the terminal decay of La Serenissima was revealed in the second half of the nineteenth century. Historians and delvers in archives are happy to compile the usual check-list of political and economic causes: their book-worn fingertips don't fall upon the first cause of the lagoonal ruination, which is due solely to the academic baptism of a new branch of the philosophical disciplines. With the publication of the *Aesthetics* (Frankfurt, 1750–58) of Alexander Gottlieb Baumgarten, the middle years of the eighteenth century marked the emergence of a new sensory receptor in the psychical body of the Western world: and if to every function there corresponds a dysfunction, if each organ expresses its own particular illness, then, inevitably, the Baumgartenian turning point gave rise to the efflorescence of an endless series of infirmities, degenerations and peculiar tumours in the newborn aesthetic organ.

But what risks are run by those who are exposed from dawn till dusk for decades to the *radium pulchritudinis*? What is the pathological configuration, the clinical picture of the pulchrodependent organism?

There is no need to go back over all the stages of the definitive obstruction of costive architectural embellishments in the historical centre of Venice, throughout these two centuries, in the last spaces upon which building was still possible: we need only recall its effects.

Unstoppable now is the blight of Venetians, who currently number barely seventy thousand emaciated surviving units. The inhabitants of Venice are *serenissimi*, not simply serene. Just think: that *-issimi* crashes through the concept of serenity, infects the idea of placid wisdom, lends it emphasis by referring to a state of morbid quietism. *Serenissimi*: it amounts to saying biochemically ecstatic, endemically stupefied, intoxicated on epiphany, made of *claritas*, addicts of the pulchro-fix.

Thank heavens, then, for the scaffolding that guarantees periodic moratoria on those highly dangerous nuclear façades. 'The eye needs to see objects few at a time, and with certain intervals or smooth patches that may bear the name of rests,' Agostino Fantastici, a Sienese architect in the early years of the nineteenth century, wrote wisely in his *Architectural Vocabulary*. This *rest*, in Fantasticinian terms, was granted to Venetian eyes, until recently, by packing the Ca' d'Oro away in a box for years and years. The pupil overtaxed by the *palazzi* of the Grand Canal was able to pause on the vertical landing of the wooden pseudo-façade, to enjoy the *interval*, to skate across the *smooth path* of those planed wooden laths. How restorative it was to contemplate the restoration of the façade of the Church of the Barefoot Friars, covered for months on end by scaffolding wrapped in light grey plastic! On windy days the synthetic fabric wrinkles in waves that billow from one side to the other: like an upright swimming-pool, a perpendicular pond.

Sadly we would have to admit that there are façades so pulchroactive as to be unwrappable. Christo, the Bulgarian artist who has based his entire career on the application on a vast scale of Man Ray's *Enigma of Isidore Ducasse*, might be able to pack away such a mass of pulchroactivity. The innocent are delighted because the directors of the restoration have seen to it that the façades of the Ca' Foscari and the Torre dell'Orologio are covered in such a way as to offer the tourists at least a simulacrum throughout the period of work. They don't know what really happened: the façades exuded their powerful image on to the surface of the enveloping canvas!

But the most serious case has been identified in San Marco. For some years the Doge's Palace has been covered by rather pretty screens, which not only reproduce the façade of the Palace in a colossal blow-up, but also risk swashbuckling *trompe-l'oeil* images of the interiors of the rooms, the paintings in which La Serenissima receives tributes in cornucopias from Neptune. The visible expedient is obtained through simulated gaps in the walls, as though the outside of the Palace had been struck by a devastating cannon shot, allowing glimpses and perspectives of the interior. Everyone, Venetians and tourists, is complimented by this consolation – false but rather skilful – for the long visual censorship of the restorations. I alone know that those enormous holes on the tarpaulins were not premeditated: it is the image of the Palace that is exploding! An unheard-of phenomenon, which makes the oozing of the image of Ca' Foscari or the Torre dell'Orologio pale into insignificance. When attempts were made to chain the pulchroactive gigaradium of the Palace, the reaction was terrifying. Such is the constipation of pulchroactivity within the roseate ducal box, such the stratification of images contained within, that the one has passed through the other, bursting like swellings or explosions, like visual thunderclaps, sundering not only the miserable consistency of the restorational canvas, but the very containing skin of the image of the façade.

Save our eyes, god of visions!

· *the bridge of gums*

COMING DOWN THE STEPS of the Ponte del Vinante, at the opening of the *sottoportico*, the eye is startled by a curious spectacle: some years ago, rather than spitting it into the canal, a passer-by stuck a piece of chewing gum to the wall at arm's length above his head. I have been unable to ascertain whether the current proliferation of chewing gums attached to the plaster is down to a phenomenon of reciprocal emulation on the part of casual ruminating pedestrians, or whether it might not be the formidable catarrhal labour of a single insane splodger.

Perhaps a more accurate examination of the finger-prints pressed into the gum by the applying thumb might resolve the mystery. So imagine this meticulous student of the professional institute of geometricians, or this maritime agency employee, on his way to school or the office each morning, and each time he passes beneath the passageway he glues to the wall a syllable of material kneaded and imbued with his humours, with an impasto stroke he marks the plaster with a fascinating diary of his own secretions, the seal of sucked sealing wax expressing the weekday feeling of a flavourless life.

It would be truly impressive one day to recognise it as a finished work, a grandiose Doublemint Auto-biography, a Berry-Splash Triumph, a sesquipedalian Apotheosis of Wrigley, more effective than any Warholian reflection on late capitalism.

Or might he not, our unknown chiclet-squasher, be a punctilious pointilliste, an innovative gum-Arabic follower of Seurat? A little patience, and the apparently chance agglomeration will gradually reveal a calculated design, a planned figuration, until every latex splat declares its essential position within the highly detailed, visionary pollen-clump; then even the most crumbling tamarind fleck, the most peripheral juicy-fruit smudge will acquire meaning in the picture: the pupil of Aphrodite, for example, or perhaps the little toenail of the Virgin.

Already, standing on the steps of the Ponte del Vinante, I try helplessly to follow the thread of the argument from one point to the next: I vainly connect, unify, join, trace navigation routes in the pebbled map of the oceanic archipelago, I secrete frail cobwebs like those of a drunken spider, I sketch sharp-edged caricatures to give this incongruous constellation an aquiline profile, I draw angular squiggles, run my biro along the unbroken meanderings of a risible Coded Path without alpha or omega, I paint a meaningless What's It Going To Be? in the enigmatic dotted inlay.

Has our unknown blob-painter chewed and rechewed each gum until he obtained the chromatic gradation required by his art? What mean mortals we are, pressing our Hubba-Bubbas to our taste buds to extenuate their vulgar gustatory essence! Our master-mosaicist doesn't care about flavours: he masticates Pure Colour! His tongue is a mortar! His oral cavity a masticatory paint shop! His palate is a palette, his molar a pestle, kneading and blending synaesthetic tones, unimagined flavoursome shades, he softens the rosy carnality of raspberry with the exsanguinated pallor of yoghurt stripe, he revives the jaundiced caoutchouc of banana with a vigorous Vigorsol of mango and grapefruit.

Perhaps not even the traces of his canines are gratuitous, still visible on the gums stuck to the plaster: one day even the dental imprints, the thumbprint cavities will have a microbic nanorelief, a puzzle of scratches, a chisel of tiny traces, a burin of nibbles, a swarm of rusticated valleys that will enrich with its reverberations the Icon, the Imago assembled by what for now seems only a rainbow rabble. The resinous material disquiet of the surfaces will capture the light in the drape of a dress, spill it out on a pillowed complexion, reflect it in the glassy sheen of an eyedrop.

Whatever the truth of the matter may be, whether this is the work of an individual or, more likely, a collective, in either case we still find ourselves beholding a postmodern mosaic masterwork, a screen of pixels, a galaxy drenched with molar tortures, a jaw-vulcanised salivary Milky Way. Amidst petals of faded spearmint, washed-out peppermint, bleached extramint, there stand out gleaming black pearls of liquorice, shocking pink strawberry, astonishing lemon yellows, amazing bubblegum blues. The Ponte del Vinante will soon be renamed the Ponte delle Gomme – the Bridge of Gums.

I think this is what happened: first of all, the application of the daily fragments is down to the brilliant initiative of a single individual. After a month he must have regurgitated and scrawled on the wall a considerable mucous patrol: out of contagious empathy, emulative challenge, metonymic mirth, the gravitational force of the concentrated material probably attracted, like a black hole, thousands of bits of chewing gum from the shadowy mouths of passers-by. I acknowledge that I find this notion the most attractive: the thought that the sticky initiative of a solitary individual, the seed chewed behind the smile of a taciturn artist might have led to the flourishing of this imposing plural fresco-in-progress.

Oh, art, art! Why must you stand on the sidelines chewing gum? Oh, you listless, flighty, silly adolescent!

· *going back to sleep in Venice*
Diogo Mainardi

WHAT I LIKE ABOUT VENICE is the blocked canal, the deserted museum, the church closed for restoration, the sweaty tourist, the cinema with the smell of drains. I like it when a young entrepreneur opens a new bar and it fails almost immediately. I like it when the plaster fragments from a run-down palazzo fall on the head of someone in the middle of the street or when a rat manages to gnaw through the fibre-optic cables.

For me, Venice is the celebration of motionlessness. It's like living in one of those welcoming religious sects in which even today they travel by horse and cart and the children die of measles because they're forbidden to use medicine. I don't think children die of measles in Venice, that would be too much to ask.

Venice represents the refusal to accept any form of innovation. So total is this refusal that not even man's most primordial inventions have managed to assert themselves here. Fire, because the city is surrounded by water. The wheel, for obvious reasons. Venetians would rather live in the branches of the trees, if there were any.

Herein lies the absolute superiority of Venice over other places. The city remains always immobile, it opposes all the little novelties that usually fill people's lives. In fact, in Venice you can't try to hide your inner void behind meaningless daily upsets, because here daily life doesn't change, it doesn't allow anyone to mask the poverty of his own existence.

Not that this awareness leads in the end to any great traumas. Certainly, the Venetians get very irritated, but their desperation is no more unbearable than anyone else's. Perhaps the opposite occurs. From childhood they learn to live with their own powerlessness, in a state of philosophical acceptance of their nullity.

For a writer such as myself, who does nothing but reassert my own nullity and other people's, there couldn't be a better place in the world. Since I moved to Venice, eight years ago, I have called into question all possible faith in human progress, in individual development.

Now I feel cornered by Venetian torpor. I will never be able to leave here. The city has a sedative effect on me. Sometimes I wake up with a great desire to readapt myself to an active role in the world, but luckily I go back to sleep a couple of seconds later.

There can be no better place than this.